THE RED EARL

The Red Earl

The Extraordinary Life of the 16th Earl of Huntingdon

Selina Hastings

BLOOMSBURY

LONDON • NEW DELHI • NEW YORK • SYDNEY

First published in Great Britain 2014

Copyright © Selina Hastings, 2014

The moral right of the author has been asserted

A Continuum book

Bloomsbury Publishing Plc
50 Bedford Square
London WC1B 3DP

www.bloomsbury.com

Bloomsbury is a trademark of Bloomsbury Publishing Plc

Bloomsbury Publishing, London, New Delhi, New York and Sydney

A CIP record for this book is available from the British Library.

ISBN 978-1-4081-8736-4

10 9 8 7 6 5 4 3 2 1

Typeset by Fakenham Prepress Solutions, Fakenham, Norfolk NR21 8NN

Printed and bound in Great Britain by CPI Group (UK) Ltd, Croydon CR0 4YY

MIX
Paper from
responsible sources
FSC
www.fsc.org
FSC® C020471

To my sister,
Caroline Harriet Shackleton
with my love

Contents

Preface

By the time I came to know him, the extraordinary events of my father's early life were long in the past. My mother was his second wife, and the two of them led a mutually agreeable existence in which only occasional reference was made to the colourful adventures that had taken place so many years ago. In most respects my father in middle age appeared a typical representative of his time and class, sober-suited, affable and courteous, clearly enjoying his mildly hedonistic way of life. Yet as I was to discover, when a young man he had defied centuries of tradition and consistently enraged his ultra-conservative parents. In his early twenties, without a word to his family, he had made a runaway marriage to a woman whom no decent, well-born Englishman would seriously consider for a wife. The two of them escaped to distant and exotic parts of the world, mixing with people whom my grandmother, very conscious of her aristocratic status, frankly described as '*scum*'.

An only son, heir to an ancient but under-funded earldom, my father had naturally been expected to restore the family fortunes by marrying well and settling down to a life mainly devoted to hunting. Instead he chose a career as an artist, and in his early twenties disappeared without warning, first to Australia, then to the South Seas. Here, he and his difficult, devoted wife led an idyllic existence on their paradisal island, until a bizarre accident forced them to leave the tropics for ever. In 1930, on their way back to England, they stopped in California where they were to spend nearly a year. During this period my father continued to paint while also enjoying an unusually varied social life, with

Hollywood stars such as Charlie Chaplin and Douglas Fairbanks on the one hand, and on the other a group of dissident intellectuals, Lincoln Steffens, Erskine Scott Wood and the distinguished poet Robinson Jeffers.

While in San Francisco for a few days my father saw in the paper a notice of an exhibition of paintings by the famous Mexican muralist, Diego Rivera. Overwhelmed by the work on show, he somehow engineered an introduction to Rivera himself, who, astonishingly, agreed to take him on as an assistant. For the next nearly four years my father lived and worked at close quarters with Rivera and with his wife, Frida Kahlo, first in San Francisco, then Detroit, and finally Mexico City. It was a friendship and an experience that remained central to his being, with Rivera's artistic creed and communist philosophy profoundly influencing his thinking for the rest of his life. When eventually he returned home it was to be faced with fighting on all fronts: in Spain during the Civil War; in England with his parents, infuriated by their son's betrayal of his family and class; and lastly with his wife, who was determined to keep him locked into a marriage from which by now he was desperate to escape.

I am well aware that I am far from my father's ideal biographer, politically obtuse and with only an elementary understanding of the visual arts. And yet his is a story that should be told. Looking back, it seems strange that in all the years I knew him my father so rarely talked about his past. My attempts long after his death to uncover his remarkable history have been frequently frustrating, but also revelatory. Mild-mannered and unfailingly polite, my father somehow succeeded in having his way in almost everything. I can't help feeling glad that he overturned hereditary expectation, and in place of the sporting Tory peer, straight out of Surtees, he evolved instead into this complex, mysterious figure almost impossible to pin down.

From Sherwood Forest to Sharavogue

When my sister and I were small we saw very little of my father. I just remember him as an occasional presence, distant but benign, bestowing a vague smile and patting us on the head as we passed him on the stairs. I was born a month before the end of the war, my sister in June the following year, and our earliest childhood was spent in the country, in Dorset. We lived in a beautiful grey-stone house with a trout stream at the bottom of the garden, and our nursery world consisted of a nanny and nursery-maid and, at one remove, of my mother, inseparably attached to her three long-haired dachshunds, Brenda, Johnnie and Max. My father, who worked in London all week, came down only at weekends, and I have no memory of him during that period of my life.

Shortly before I turned five we moved to London, the reason being, as my mother told me later, that my father hated being away from her and found the commuting wearisome. But again there was little communal existence: my parents lived in an apartment in Albany, in Piccadilly, where children are not allowed, while we for a year or so were settled, with cook and nursery governess, in a small house with a garden on the outskirts of Richmond. Here we attended a little dame school run by two spinster sisters, Miss Lee and Miss Katie Lee, and my parents came down to see us most weekends. I can just recall my father at this stage, although the picture is indistinct: that of a tall, moustachioed figure in a dark suit, and, as before, amiable but remote. On one occasion he bent down to make some kindly remark and I looked up in bafflement: surrounded by women, I had never heard a man speak before and I was unable to understand a single word he said. Understandably, he was not encouraged to repeat the attempt, and it was some years before he and I became better acquainted.

In the early stages of growing up one accepts almost everything as normal, and I never questioned this detached and strangely formal relationship. It wasn't until I was well into my teens that I came to know my father a little, and indeed to love him dearly. I also began to discover just how extraordinary his early life had been. His career had followed an unusual trajectory; exotic, adventurous, and in emotional terms frequently explosive. In almost every respect it could have been designed to defy the rooted traditions of that line of unenquiring English aristocracy into which he had been born. As an only son, the heir to an earldom, his path had been clearly set out, but at almost every turn he had deliberately flouted expectation. Occasionally he would tell us part of his story, but it was a long time before I learnt to what extent his own early childhood had left him unaware of the normal conduits of affection between parent and child.

Had he been born a mere eight days earlier my father would have been a Victorian: the old Queen died on 22 January 1901; he arrived, at 10 Grosvenor Square in London, on 30 January. The world in which he grew up was still entrenched in the nineteenth century. In the distant past the Hastings family had been distinguished, taking a prominent role in national affairs, but recent generations had retired into a peaceful obscurity, the family characterised by a genial philistinism and a consuming passion for horses and hunting: Hastingses were happiest when mounted and preferably in pursuit of prey.

Further back there was a more romantic history, beginning, according to family legend, with a Comte d'Eu, who came over with the Conqueror in 1066, a Plantagenet who was given the name Hastings after the battle, an honour later upgraded to a barony by Edward III. A later Lord Hastings was beheaded by Richard III, an unkindness redressed by Henry VIII who conferred on the son of the executed Baron the Earldom of Huntingdon.

During the reign of Elizabeth I the third Earl, who had wisely renounced his Plantagenet claim to the throne, was appointed guardian of Mary, Queen of Scots. The pretty Queen was kept a prisoner at his castle at Ashby-de-la-Zouch in Leicestershire – until Elizabeth was informed by her spies that 'Huntingdon was becoming too attracted to the lady'. Mary was promptly removed to Fotheringay Castle, and his lordship otherwise employed in a demanding job as Governor of the North of England. His daughter, Lady Mary Hastings, a famous beauty, was put forward as a prospective bride for Ivan the Terrible, Emperor of Russia, but the young woman was so appalled by the prospect that she implored the Queen to intercede. The alliance did not take place, and Lady Mary died unmarried.

My father loved these stories, and recounted them with relish, not always particularly interested in sticking strictly to historical fact. His favourite was a dubious tradition that identified Robin Hood as an Earl of Huntingdon. That this legendary figure was almost certainly fictitious troubled my father not at all. If asked for evidence he would quote the lines to be found on Robin Hood's gravestone at Kirklees Priory in Yorkshire:

Hear undernead dis laitl stean
Lais Robert Earl of Huntingtun
Near arcir der as hie sa geud
An pipl kauld im Robin Heud.
Sic utlaws as hi an is men
Vil England nivr si agen.[1]
Obiit 24 Kal Dekembris 1247

---

[1] Here underneath this little stone
Lies Robert Earl of Huntingdon
No archer was as he so good
And people called him Robin Hood.
Such outlaws as he and his men
Will England never see again.

So keen was the family on this romantic connection that many a male child was inflicted with the name: my great-uncle Aubrey Hastings, for instance, was christened Aubrey Theophilus Robin Hood, while his son, Peter Robin Hood, named his three sons William Edward Robin Hood, Simon Aubrey Robin Hood, John Peter Robin Hood. The present Earl, born in 1948, is William Edward Robin Hood, who further followed Hastings tradition in a love of horses, becoming racehorse trainer to the Queen.

Like his predecessors, my father, too, was brought up in the saddle. His father, Warner Huntingdon, lived for horses and hounds, as Warner's father and grandfather had done before him. Warner's mother, Wilmot, was the granddaughter of a well-to-do Anglo-Irish peer, Lord Rossmore, and on her marriage in 1867 she brought with her as dowry a couple of modest estates in Ireland, one of which, in King's County, was fortunately possessed of some of the best hunting in the country. Here, at Sharavogue, the Hastingses settled down to an agreeable way of life single-mindedly devoted to the chase.

An affable man of unfailing courtesy and charm, Warner, my grandfather, gave little outward indication of his tenaciousness and determination. Nothing and no one was allowed to get in the way of his annual routine, entirely focused on horses and the pursuit of the fox. His father, Francis Huntingdon, had been the same, a keen polo player, Master of the King's County and Ormond Foxhounds, admiringly depicted in the local press as 'one of the straightest riders who ever followed a pack'. Francis's wife, Wilmot, and his eight children organised their lives entirely around the hunting season, with Wilmot approvingly described as 'more happy in the saddle, especially when in full career after the hounds, than anywhere else'.

Of Francis's three sons, all followed in their father's hoof-prints, with the youngest, Aubrey Hastings, famous as a three-times winner of the Grand National. Perhaps appropriately, Aubrey died with his foot in the stirrup, felled by a heart attack while mounting his pony during a game of polo. His funeral was attended by a handful of titled relations and by over 40 stable lads and jockeys. His five sisters, the Ladies Constance, Ileene, Ierne, Rowena and Noreen, were all spirited girls, 'bred to the saddle ... fearless and first-rate to hounds ... [and] even when still in the schoolroom, [they] were in the habit of spending long hours daily in the hunting-field'.

Warner, the eldest son, first went out with hounds at the age of three; at 14 he kept two packs of beagles, and by 16 was not only hunting but playing polo, riding in point-to-points and steeple-chasing. During his lifetime Warner became in turn Master of the Ormond Hunt, the East Galway, the North Staffordshire, and of the prestigious Atherstone in Leicestershire. (He was offered the even more famous Quorn but turned it down when he learned to his disgust that the Master was a figurehead only, the actual day-to-day hunting left in charge of a professional huntsman.) With hunting in the winter and polo in the summer, his early life was spent almost continually in the saddle; later on, as well as hunting in Ireland, he would cross to England every year for the hunting season there; on the few occasions when his health let him down, he insisted on following the field as far as possible by car. He made a fine, moustachioed figure in his cap and scarlet coat, always photographed astride, magnificently mounted, riding crop in hand, surrounded by his huntsman and his pack of hounds. 'The Earl of Huntingdon', The *Bystander* noted approvingly in 1911, 'is now as fine an amateur huntsman as exists ... He is very popular with all classes ... and hounds simply love him.'

Of course there were times when this equestrian idyll had temporarily to be abandoned. As a boy of 12, Warner was sent to Dublin to serve for a year as a page at the viceregal court, and shortly afterwards was dispatched to school in England. Here he was wretchedly unhappy, painfully missing his mother, a loving, sweet-natured and deeply religious woman. In 1883, at the age of 14, he wrote to her,

My own dearest Mother,

Thanks so much for your letters & the awfully nice book. This is an awful change after home so different I do feel so sad & horrible … This is an awful hole. I will never live through this term.

Much love ever
Your very affec loving
Your Hastings

At 15 he left on one of the only two trips he ever made abroad, going with a tutor to Canada, where the highlights were visits to the Niagara Falls and to the first ever Kennel Club dog show, which took place in Toronto. It was not long after his return home that his father died, and Warner at the age of 16 succeeded to the earldom.

Francis Huntingdon's death in 1885, after a short illness, came as a great shock to the family – followed by an even greater shock when it was discovered what a parlous situation they were in financially. Francis, feckless and impractical, had gone through much of his wife's fortune, and now Wilmot and her eight children found themselves in the care of a trustee, who was charged with controlling household expenses and administering the Irish estates, Sharavogue and Derrykeel in King's County, Clashmore in County Waterford.

This was not the first time the family had found itself in difficulties. From a position of formidable wealth and power in the Tudor period, more recent generations of Hastingses had fallen on hard times. The decline was mainly due to an unfortunate reverse during the reign of George III, when it was mistakenly believed the title had died out; the extensive estates in Leicestershire and elsewhere, together with all money and possessions, had passed to a ducal cousin who, when the rightful claimant to the earldom at last came forward, declined to return them.

By time-honoured tradition, the most respectable method of regaining status was to marry money, but in this the Hastingses had proved only moderately successful. Indeed Francis himself had made the most advantageous match in marrying Wilmot Westenra, whose mother, a Miss Daubuz, originally of Portuguese extraction, had brought with her a handsome dowry. It was from Wilmot's family that the Irish estates had passed into Hastings hands, property that, although it had not made them rich, at least provided enough on which to live comfortably and to hunt.

Unfortunately, the trustee in charge of the estate during Warner's minority turned out to be a crook. Within a matter of months, he had siphoned off most of the money for himself and disappeared, leaving Warner, his mother and siblings still resident at Sharavogue but with little to live on. Luckily they were rescued by the kind intervention of a near relation.

One of Warner's cousins had somehow succeeded in engineering an engagement between his nice but plain daughter, Kathleen, and the Duke of Newcastle. Warner, invited to the wedding, started talking to the new Duchess, always known as 'Tata', the two of them quickly discovering a shared interest in horses and dogs (fox terriers were Tata's particular passion). From that day on they became firm friends, with Warner a frequent guest both at parties in London and at Clumber, the Duke's great house in Nottinghamshire. It was always believed that it was Tata, famously warm-hearted, who helped the Hastings family financially. Crucially for Warner, it was at the Newcastles' London house that he met his future wife.

Maud Wilson was the daughter of a very rich man, a fact which must have had at least some bearing on Warner Huntingdon's initial interest when they first met with the Newcastles. No beauty, but confident, lively, a good dancer and expensively dressed, Maud was clearly a rewarding companion at an evening party. With his precarious finances, Warner was in no position to waste time, nor did he wish to stay away any longer than he could help from his horses and hounds at Sharavogue. The engagement was announced in *The Times* on 16 April 1892, and the couple were married at the fashionable St George's, Hanover Square, on 11 June.

The wedding was followed by a magnificent reception for 300 guests at the Wilsons' house in Grosvenor Square, where among the many wedding presents on display was one from the bridegroom to his bride, a silver-mounted hunting-crop. After an elaborate luncheon the newly married pair departed to spend their honeymoon at Clumber, generously put at their disposal by Tata. Three weeks later Warner took his bride home to Sharavogue where, to celebrate the new Countess's arrival, a party was given for the tenantry – dinner for 160 in the coach-house, followed by dancing in the granary. 'The dishes were numerous, everything in season being on the menu, and there was abundance of good cheer', the *King's County Chronicle* reported. A toast was proposed by one of the farmers, who declared 'he had known generations of the Hastings, and would say that there never was a nobleman more popular or better liked by the tenantry than the young lord who so generously entertained them that night'.

Sharavogue must have appeared dismayingly shabby to its new mistress, accustomed to the luxury and comfort of her father's Mayfair mansion with its staff of over 40 servants. Maud's father was a remarkable man. Sir Samuel Wilson, born in 1832, was the youngest of six sons of a prosperous farmer from County Antrim in Ireland. At the age of 20 he had emigrated to Australia, and beginning with very little he became immensely rich from sheep-farming in Queensland, Victoria and New South Wales. His stations covered millions of acres, and he bred the purest Merino stock, winning numerous prizes for his wool in London and Paris. He bought Ercildoune, a fine house and estate near Ballarat, Victoria, where he lived with his wife, Jeannie Campbell, daughter of another prosperous member of the squattocracy, and their seven children.

Red-haired and hot-tempered, he was more feared than loved: when after his death his widow was asked if she would marry again, she replied with a grimace, 'Once bitten, twice shy!' Samuel, proud of his standing as a pre-Gold Rush pastoralist, made not only a great fortune but a distinguished career for himself in politics, elected a member first of the Legislative Assembly, then of the Legislative Council of Victoria. He was a member of the exclusive Melbourne Club in Collins Street, gave prodigious amounts to charity, including the then enormous sum of £30,000 towards the building of Melbourne University, and was knighted in 1875. Socially ambitious, Sir Sam amused the more irreverent of his colonial compeers with his superior airs; he was thought to act too much the nabob and behind his back they called him 'Sir Sham'.

In 1881, when Maud was 13, Sir Sam brought his family to England. As well as the house in Grosvenor Square he rented Hughenden Manor in Buckinghamshire, which had recently been owned by Benjamin Disraeli. In 1886 he was elected Conservative member for Portsmouth, although he made little impact in the House of Commons, preferring to dedicate most of his energies to social climbing and to finding titled spouses for his children. In this he enjoyed two notable successes: first the marriage of his eldest son, Gordon, to Lady Sarah Spencer-Churchill, Winston Churchill's aunt and daughter of the Duke of Marlborough; and second, less than a year later, that of his daughter, Maud, to the Earl of Huntingdon.

Maud was 24 when she married, reportedly on the rebound after a failed romance. She had made her début six long years earlier, and so delighted was Maud's father with the social standing of her fiancé that he gave her a dowry of £5,000 a year (the equivalent now of about £750,000) as well as a share in one of the most profitable of his sheep-farms, the Yanko in New South Wales.

Yet, worldly considerations apart, the young Huntingdons must have seemed singularly ill-matched. Warner loathed social life, disliked the town, and after the wedding could hardly wait to return to Ireland to continue his sporting pursuits. The two great passions of Maud's life were parties and the theatre. In Australia her girlhood ambition had been to go on the stage, which of course was out of the question; however, once arrived in England she had high hopes of taking a leading role in London society. Such hopes were soon disappointed, and during the next decade the Countess of Huntingdon appeared only twice yearly in the capital, her arrival at Grosvenor Square duly recorded in the Court Circular in *The Times*, as was her presence at various grand social gatherings, most notably those private theatricals that were such a popular pastime of the period. The rest of the year she and her husband spent mostly at Sharavogue. The one time during his long marriage that Warner was persuaded to go abroad was in 1899 when he accompanied his wife on the only return visit she ever made to Australia.

Maud was bossy, quick-tempered, supremely self-assured and possessed of enormous reserves of physical energy; she liked to be active, in command, and surrounded by plenty of people – people, it goes without saying, of an acceptable social standing. (She had been disappointed to learn that her husband had refused the superior title of marquess: when soon after his father's death he was informed he had a claim to the marquessate of Hastings, Warner declined to pursue it: 'marquess' was a French title and relatively new, he said dismissively, whereas an earldom was ancient and English.)

Warner was quietly spoken and invariably polite: he rarely lost his temper, and if he disliked someone they never knew it. Happiest in his own company or with one or two old friends, he attended social occasions only under pressure, and yet he was extremely popular in the county, known at every level of society for his 'genuine amiability & friendship'. Affable and easy-going, it was Warner, however, who was the dominant partner in the marriage. Underneath his gentle courtesy was a ruthless streak that ensured he nearly always won his own way, a formidable strength of character later to be inherited by his only son.

Despite their very different temperaments, however, the couple quickly found a congenial method of mutual existence, and although Warner had little interest in people and parties, Maud for her part was a fine horsewoman and enjoyed riding to hounds, her pluck and vigour much admired among the hunting fraternity. In other areas she was left to do very much as she pleased, energetically devoting herself to entertaining the county and staging elaborate *tableaux vivants*, posed by the young ladies and gentlemen of the neighbouring Ascendancy families. Only 18 months after Maud came to live at Sharavogue, Wilmot, Warner's mother, died – 'hunting has been postponed as a mark of respect', the local paper reported when announcing 'the mournful intelligence' – and from then on Maud was queen of her domain.

Sharavogue – the name means 'bitter land' – is situated halfway along the road between Roscrea and Parsonstown (now Birr). Both towns possess ancient castles, but whereas the castle at Roscrea had long been a ruin, Parsonstown, an elegant Georgian settlement of wide streets and fine municipal buildings, was dominated by the magnificent Birr Castle, family seat of the Earls of Rosse. The tiny hamlet of Sharavogue lies on the edge of the Bog of Allen, surrounded by pleasant, well-farmed country, gently undulating and characterised by meadows and small copses, by bushy hedgerows and fast-running streams. The Huntingdons' estate was modest in size, covering an area of just under 500 acres, the entrance to it marked by a pair of lodge-keepers' cottages which stood on either side of the gates at the end the drive.

Built in the 1820s, Sharavogue was a gabled, two-storey manor of no particular distinction, slightly dilapidated in appearance, with its walls heavily draped in creeper. A shady garden surrounded the house on three sides, and as well as an orchard and farmyard there were kennels for the hounds and extensive stabling for over 30 hunters as well as polo ponies and carriage horses – including the four handsome greys which drew the massive old family coach. Surrounding this well-populated nucleus was a small, tree-studded park in which were a couple of paddocks, a polo ground, a race-track, and at the furthest boundary the ivy-covered ruins of the ancient castle of Rathmore.

Indoors, the house was comfortable and slightly dilapidated, the ground floor a series of modestly proportioned rooms furnished with faded fabrics and well-used sofas and chairs. A favourite retreat for Warner, as it had been for his father and grandfather before him, was a cosy parlour to the right of the hall, its walls

hung with dozens of equine pictures, the pride of the collection
four magnificent paintings of noble steeds by the famous John
Ferneley. In among them were a few family portraits, including
a handsome miniature of Warner himself in his red coat, and
several pictures of hounds, both individually and in groups.

Here and throughout the house were other mementos of
the chase: inkwells made from horses' hooves, deer-foot letter-
openers, horsetail fly-whisks, silver ashtrays ornamented with a
tiny fox's face and brush; corridors were hung with group photographs of hunt servants from the recent past, while at intervals
furry foxes' masks snarled down from wooden shields on which
were recorded the date and place of the kill. In the centre of the
dining-table stood a silver hound on a silver plinth; a miniature
fox's head, also in silver, held sugar, while crystal pheasants with
golden plumage stood sentinel at each of the four corners.

Comfortable the house may have been, but Maud, once she
was in charge, could hardly wait to expand and improve. She
and Warner moved out to a property only a few miles away
while the distinguished Dublin architect, Sir Thomas Deane, was
commissioned to undertake a radical reconstruction. Walls were
torn down, new rooms were added while others were significantly enlarged, with the smoky little parlour leading off the hall
swallowed up into a grand new reception room. The hall itself was
doubled in length and lined in carved black oak in the Jacobean
style, tall oriel windows were installed; the narrow old staircase
was completely demolished and replaced by a massive new one,
also in carved oak, leading up to an elegantly arcaded first floor.
Two bathrooms were put in, several new bedrooms, and an entirely
new wing built for the servants. For the first time electric light and
central heating largely took the place of oil lamps and open fires,
and once the building work was finished the entire house was
reboarded, replastered and repainted, chairs were re-covered, new
carpet laid and windows hung with curtains of a rich silk plush.

The motto carved over the front door at Sharavogue, 'Céad mile
fáilte' ('a hundred thousand welcomes'), can never have appeared

more appropriate, for with the renovations complete, Maud lost no time in launching out on an ambitious social life. As well as taking over the traditional fixtures for polo, tennis, golf and cricket, Maud organised an intensive programme of shooting lunches and hunt balls, of dinner parties and informal dances, croquet tournaments, summer fêtes and charity bazaars. And whenever opportunity offered she would seize the chance to indulge her passion for the theatre: Lady Huntingdon's amateur productions soon became a popular feature among the local gentry, with Maud vigorously in charge, designing and directing a series of 'musical living pictures'.

In these, usually staged before an invited audience in the drawing-room at Sharavogue, the young ladies and gentlemen of the county posed, with musical accompaniment, in a series of tableaux. The curtain would rise, for instance, on a love-sick Dante gazing at Beatrice, or on Sir John Millais's picture of 'Bubbles', or perhaps on the three witches from *Macbeth*. These entertainments were greatly relished, eagerly attended by young and old alike, among the regular patrons the Countess of Rosse, Maud's neighbour from Birr Castle, the Countess of Fingall from Killeen, and Warner's cousin, Lady Rossmore.

It was Lady Rossmore who in 1896 presented Maud at the viceregal court at Dublin Castle. For Maud, largely denied the sophisticated society of London, Dublin was the next best thing, and the Lord Lieutenant's magnificently formal style of entertaining delighted her. In Dublin Castle, with its richly decorated State Apartments, its Banqueting Hall and Throne Room, with its footmen in scarlet and gold, was where she felt she belonged. Determined to make the most of the short Dublin season, Maud took every opportunity to attend Levees and Drawing Rooms, banquets and balls, dancing till the early hours beneath the great Waterford chandelier in the gilded and galleried St Patrick's Hall. While Warner for the most part remained contentedly at home with his horses and dogs, Maud would stay in Dublin with her closest ally, the clever, pretty and very vain Countess of Fingall. Daisy Fingall, like Maud, loved high society, and the two of them, dressed up to the nines, were frequent guests at the Castle. On one occasion, Maud blazed forth at a Drawing Room in a ball dress of pale blue satin embroidered in silver, the train decorated with lace and gardenias, wearing a diamond necklace and tiara, several ropes of pearls, and carrying a bough of gardenias tied with a blue satin ribbon.

In August 1902 Maud and Daisy Fingall went over to London for the coronation of Edward VII, both their husbands, dismayed by the prospect of lengthy ceremonies and intensive socialising, having refused to attend. On the morning of the coronation itself, the two of them in full court dress left Grosvenor Square at 6.00 am, rumbling along the early-morning streets in the immensely ornate Wilson family carriage. Arrived at the Abbey, they discreetly checked each other's appearance. 'Lady Huntingdon wore a magnificent tiara,' Daisy Fingall recalled, 'and I remember straightening it for her when we got to the Abbey, after the swaying of the carriage which had set it awry … We wore our trains as cloaks and carried our coronets on our knees … It was all very impressive and awe-inspiring.'

Lady Fingall's was exactly the kind of society that Maud most enjoyed. Although her father had made such a remarkable career, Maud in later life came to feel a little ashamed of her colonial origins. She maintained few links with Australia, and outside her immediate family rarely referred to her antipodean childhood. In the early years of her marriage, however, she felt no such embarrassment, even, in 1903, appearing at a charity ball gorgeously arrayed as the Spirit of Australia.

One of several acquaintances from her early years with whom she had kept in regular contact was the great soprano Nellie Melba. The two had known each other as girls, Melba, like Maud, having been brought up near Melbourne, and after making her name and a large fortune Melba had rented Sir Sam's old house, Ercildoune. When in London, she and Maud often collaborated, Melba singing at private concerts organised by Maud, the two of them manning stalls together at fashionable charity bazaars.

In June 1895, after appearing in *Faust* at Covent Garden, Melba came to stay at Sharavogue. By an odd coincidence, within days of her arrival came news of the death of Sir Sam, recently returned to England from a visit to Australia. After a short service at Grosvenor Square, he was buried beneath an imposing funerary monument in the cemetery at Kensal Green.

From the day of her wedding, unspoken but clearly understood was the fact that Maud's primary purpose in life was to produce an heir to the title. Disappointingly, the first three children were girls, Kathleen, born in 1893, Norah in 1894, and (in a familial gesture towards Sherwood Forest) Marian in 1895. Six years then passed until finally, on 30 January 1901, the longed-for son was born.

The baby's arrival could hardly have been better timed. For years both parents had longed for a boy, and his birth coincided with an anxious period when good news was particularly welcome. The second Boer War had broken out in 1899, and all four of Maud's brothers had volunteered for South Africa; one, Wilfrid, was killed, while another, Clarence, suffered wounds from which he never fully recovered. Herbert, the youngest, was mentioned in dispatches, but it was the eldest brother, Gordon Wilson, whose experience was most often recounted within the family.

Gordon and his wife, Sarah, the Duke of Marlborough's daughter, were already in South Africa when war was declared, Gordon as ADC to Baden-Powell, the commanding officer at Mafeking. When the siege began, Lady Sarah started filing stories from inside the besieged city for the *Daily Mail*, thus quickly winning a sensational reputation for herself. Privately the Hastings family had always found Lady Sarah something of a trial: very conscious of her family's ducal status, Lady Sarah, who with her bulging eyes looked like a bad-tempered Pekinese, was bossy and patronising, with a sarcastic laugh that made them cringe. During the siege she was taken prisoner by the Boers, but, said my father drily when telling the tale, the Boers quickly realised they'd bitten off more than they could chew and returned her unharmed in less than a day.

In Ireland Warner played a rather less challenging role in the war. As a young man he had joined the 3rd Battalion of the Prince of Wales's Leinster Regiment, stationed in Parsonstown, eventually reaching the rank of Lieutenant-Colonel. Although military activity could never compete with the hunting field, Warner undoubtedly took his duties seriously and was now fully occupied helping muster over half the garrison for deployment to South Africa in March 1900. It was a sombre period at Sharavogue: most of Warner's hunters were sold to the army, the playing of polo came to a halt, racing was largely abandoned, and the hunt was reduced to a minimum and barely kept going.

In preparation for her lying-in Maud went to London to stay with her mother in Grosvenor Square. As her son was born only eight days after the death of Queen Victoria, on 30 January 1901, the announcement of his birth at Sharavogue was postponed as a matter of decorum. But then one evening in the second week of February his arrival was celebrated on the estate with a lighting of bonfires, with singing and dancing, tables laden with food, beer by the cartload, and when Warner appeared he was greeted with hearty cheers and well-fuelled expressions of congratulation. Within a couple of months Maud returned to Ireland, and that autumn, as soon as the hunting season opened, the son and heir was introduced to the one component that would surely be central to his future existence. As usual the hunt assembled in front of the house: 'one of the most interesting personages on the field', the local paper reported, 'was little Lord Hastings, whose chubby face peeped out of an all-white wool and fur dress. In the arms of his nurse he was spoken to by mount after mount as they passed by, and he did not appear at all displeased by the attention showered upon him.'

For Francis John Clarence Westenra Plantagenet Hastings, always known as Jack, a name he disliked, his happiest childhood memories were of Sharavogue. Sharavogue, he said later in life, was the only home to which he ever felt truly attached. He always spoke of it fondly and treasured the few souvenirs that survived:

a small fox's mask in silver was kept on his desk, a couple of Irish hunt cartoons hung on his studio walls, and one of his favourite possessions was the great iron bell that used to toll from the stables; Sharavogue, too, was the name he gave the yacht which in later years he kept on the Beaulieu River in Hampshire.

Delighted though they were by the birth of an heir, neither of Jack's parents were much involved in his daily existence. In keeping with the custom of their class and time, children were seen only once a day by their parents, brought down by a nurse, ironed and starched, to the drawing-room after tea. Jack's earliest memories were not of his mother but of an unkind nanny who punished him by burning his hand with an iron. Fortunately his screams brought Maud running, and the woman was instantly dismissed.

In due course he was promoted from nursery to schoolroom, where he had lessons with a much-loved governess, Miss Lavington, who later became governess to the sisters of Vladimir Nabokov in Russia and then to the daughters of the Tsar. Miss Lavington was lively and kind-hearted, and used to sing to the children, accompanying herself on a mandolin gaily decorated with a thick swag of multicoloured ribbons knotted with small silver charms.

It was his three sisters, however, who were Jack's most constant companions, and it was they, Kathleen, Norah and Marian, who played with him, read to him (for Jack, as for Nabokov, Florence Upton's *Golliwogg* books were among his favourite stories), invented games in the nursery, and took him with them when they went roaming the woods and fields. Like most children, Jack and his sisters had a strong interest in the supernatural and enjoyed frightening each other with stories of ghosts and monsters, many of them well known in the locality. On the edge of the Sharavogue estate were the romantic ruins of the castle of Rathmore, overgrown with creeper, surrounded by trees and said to be haunted by a spectral vampire, the ghost of a brutal warlord who drank the blood of his captives. Only a short ride away down the road to Roscrea was Leap Castle, the approach of whose resident ghost, the tall and terrifying Elemental, half human, half goat, was heralded by an appalling stench of decomposing flesh.

Within the narrow limits available to them, the children soon became practised at evading authority, knowing just where to hide when they heard their mother coming. They revelled in their brief periods of liberty, unsupervised by nursemaids or governess, when they were free to disappear into the surrounding woods and farmland and live for a time in a world of their own. In 1927, long after the family had left Sharavogue, Norah, recalling those days, wrote to Jack, 'I returned to Sharavogue one afternoon, & spent a few solitary hours there by myself, visiting all the old haunts once again before they disappear for ever ... All the trees in Rathmore are to be cut down & the old castle pulled down, the stones to be used for fresh buildings. It has stood there since 900 ... I climbed once again the weeping beech, where I found many inscriptions, inscribed by all of us at various times ... I so often used to sit in that tree whilst time stood still listening to the birds & just existing.'[2]

Solidly Conservative, staunch members of the Church of England, both Jack's parents were naturally anxious to encourage in their son the qualities most important to themselves. They must have been gratified when, barely out of the pram, little Lord Hastings was described in the local paper as 'one of the chubbiest, liveliest two-year-old peers that could be found ... [whose] chief amusement is playing with toy horses'. And indeed Warner saw to it that almost before Jack could walk he was taught to ride, led out with the hunt at the age of five, only seven when he was present at his first kill. True to family tradition, Jack took to it at once, and years later used to say he had never found anything more exciting in life than galloping fast to hounds in close pursuit of the quarry. Shooting and fishing were also much enjoyed, and the instructive

---

[2] Norah Kilmorey to JH 6.6.27. Kilmorey collection, PRONI.

rhymes that went with them were permanently embedded in his memory:

Never never let your gun
Pointed be at anyone.
That it may unloaded be
Matters not a rap to me …

Maud for her part lost little time in enrolling the youngest member of the family in her theatrical productions. His début, at the age of four, was in a play about that distinguished Hastings ancestor, Robin Hood, written by his sister Kathleen and staged at home one Christmas. 'I was forced to stuff my ordinary clothes into Lincoln green tights,' Jack recalled. 'Then I was propelled onto the stage where I had to fall on one knee and announce "The Sheriff of Nottingham approaches!"' In another of Kathleen's productions, Jack aged seven and dressed as a fairy brought the house down with a spirited clog dance.

Perhaps unsurprisingly, Jack never felt close to his parents. They were too self-centred, too remote, and although in some ways he admired them, he felt little real affection for either. Warner was too detached a figure for him ever really to know. Once when asked if he thought his father had loved him, Jack replied, 'I don't think he did really. He was very handsome, the soul of honour, quite an ornament in the County, but to me he was rather frightening. The only things he really cared for were fox-hunting, Sharavogue and my mother – in that order.' And Maud, with her quick temper and domineering manner, was equally unapproachable.

In a brief account by my father of the family history, which I discovered only after his death, he describes his mother as 'a determined character with a strong conviction that she was always right … With good intentions she bullied her children and sadly became a figure more dreaded than loved.' Certainly by the time I met her, 'Granny Huntingdon' was a formidable old lady, notorious for her driving energy, her unassailable self-confidence and a terrifying tendency towards speaking her mind, with little regard to the sometimes devastating effect on her hearers. My grandmother died when I was only seven, and at that age I knew nothing of the rages and dramas, of the decades of internecine warfare conducted with her only son.

Undoubtedly Jack was fortunate to have three older sisters to stand between him and his parents, and it was for them that he felt the strongest bonds of affection. Dearest of all was the youngest, Marian: not only was she closest to him in age, but, inquisitive and high-spirited, she made everything fun and was unfailingly affectionate towards her little brother. Interestingly in the light of subsequent events, Marian was the least loved of all the children. After Maud had disappointed expectation by twice giving birth to girls, the doctor assured Warner that the third baby would be a boy; when this turned out not to be the case, the hostility Warner felt towards his youngest daughter was profound and remained so for the rest of his life.

For the Huntingdons, there was no question that, as their only son, Jack's future was marked out for him: a gentleman's education at Eton and Oxford; marriage to an heiress, for the family was always short of money; an undemanding career in some respectable firm in the city; and of course every spare waking moment to be spent either hunting, shooting or fishing. Jack was an angelic-looking little boy, fair-haired, with pink cheeks and blue eyes. There is a portrait of him at this age, with Fauntleroy curls, velvet suit and lace collar, looking dreamily into the middle distance, seemingly unaware of the gun he is holding in his right hand. All was set for him to follow the path his parents had planned, and nobody could have foreseen the extreme lengths to which he would go to explode their expectations.

2

'Always go where money is'

My father talked very little about his schooldays. I knew he went to Eton because from time to time he would nostalgically describe a delicious-sounding concoction called Eton Mess, involving strawberries and cream and crushed meringue. He promised to make it for us one day but somehow it never materialised. Another Eton theme was his blaming the school for his atrocious handwriting, which, he said, was the result of having to write hundreds of lines as punishment while sitting in detention: the boys were quick to realise the dreary process could be speeded up by tying six pens together – with entirely predictable results.

From his earliest days my father's hand was almost illegible, a spidery scrawl that requires more time for the reader to decipher than it can have taken him to write. Not that the content was ever very revealing: 'never put down on paper what you would mind being read out in court', he would tell my sister and me, a prescription, it seems, that he followed to the letter. In trying to uncover the events of his life, I find it a constant frustration that his correspondence is so meagre and gives so little away: I often feel I'm on the trail not of Jack Hastings, but of the Invisible Man.

Indeed, it was only when going through his papers after his death that I discovered the name of Jack's preparatory school, scrawled on a carbon application form for the Slade School of Art. Stone House in Broadstairs, Kent, where he was a pupil from 1908 to 1914, was a reputable establishment highly regarded as a feeder for the three most prestigious public schools, Eton, Harrow and Winchester. The school building was a fine Georgian house surrounded by trees and lawns which on one side sloped down to the North Sea: on a fine day the coast of France was clearly visible, and in bad weather the sound of the fog-horn on the Goodwin Sands floated mournfully ashore.

The headmaster, the Rev. William Henry Churchill, was a vigorous and engaging character, whose daily dramatic readings from the works of Dickens, Henty and Rider Haggard were much appreciated by his pupils; he also encouraged lessons in music and singing, and was a keen supporter of the concert performances of Gilbert & Sullivan at the end of term. Attendance at church services was of course obligatory, and every Sunday after chapel the little boys, in top hats and Eton jackets, walked in a crocodile by the shore, chattering to the accompanying master. It was a good school, but for a child of seven it must have been a wrenching experience to be sent across the Irish Sea to the other side of England, away from home and his sisters and Sharavogue. The single reference I found in my father's own words was in a letter written half a century later to his friend, the philosopher Bertrand Russell, in which he makes brief mention of 'my mildly unhappy years at Stone House'.[3]

Jack began his Eton career at the age of 13, only a few weeks after Britain's entry into the European war. His grandfather, Francis, had been at the school, though not, it seems, Warner; the most recent Etonian in the family was Maud's brother, Jack's Uncle Gordon, who as a schoolboy had famously helped save the life of Queen Victoria. One morning in March 1882, as the Queen in her carriage was leaving Windsor station, a madman fired a gun at her. Gordon and a friend, standing in a group of Eton boys, promptly attacked the assailant with their umbrellas, thus earning their sovereign's gratitude and considerable coverage in the local press. Gordon and his father, Sir Samuel Wilson, were subsequently invited to the Castle, and Sir Sam later commemorated his son's heroism by installing a stained-glass window depicting the event in his local church at Hughenden. Gordon went on to

---

[3] JH to Bertrand Russell 16.5.67. Bertrand Russell Archive, McMaster University.

make a distinguished military career, and as a Lieutenant-Colonel in the Royal Horse Guards left for France immediately after the outbreak of war. He was killed three months later, leading his men into action at the Battle of Ypres.

Jack's Eton career was heavily overshadowed by the war. Not only was there his Uncle Gordon's death in 1914, but another uncle, Herbert Wilson, was killed three years later at the Battle of Arras. During the holidays at Sharavogue, Jack found his father fully occupied with military duties, his position as Lieutenant-Colonel in command of the 3rd Battalion of the Prince of Wales's Leinster Regiment requiring his daily presence at the garrison in Parsonstown. At school the effects of wartime were mainly manifested in the awfulness of the food, a lack of younger masters, and rigorous training in the OTC (Officers' Training Corps). In chapel the names of old boys killed in action were read out, and once a week there was a service of intercession to pray for an Allied victory. In all, over a thousand Etonians lost their lives during the four years of the war.

Despite the horrors taking place on the other side of the Channel, however, after a while the boys grew accustomed to the grim news, managing to remain effectively cocooned in their own world of school. One of Jack's Eton contemporaries, George Orwell, wrote of this period, 'It is an instance of the horrible selfishness of children that by 1917 the war had almost ceased to affect us, except through our stomachs … to be as slack as you dared on O.T.C. parades, and to take no interest in the war, was considered a mark of enlightenment.'[4]

Records of my father's career at Eton are disappointingly sparse: he is registered as present at the compulsory OTC parades, and there are pictures of him rowing, playing cricket and in later years as a member of the Library, but his name is absent from most extra-curricular activities. He was certainly not one of those

[4] *My Country Right or Left, Folio of New Writing, Autumn 1940, Collected Essays, Journalism and Letters of George Orwell*, Sonia Orwell and Ian Angus (eds) (Secker & Warburg, 1940)

who, like another contemporary, Cyril Connolly, looked back on Eton as a Golden Age after which the rest of life inevitably proved an anticlimax. When talking about his old school in later life, however, Jack's feelings towards it were fairly benign. He had loved the beauty of the place, the jumble of medieval and Victorian buildings, the cobbled School Yard with the statue of the school's founder, Henry VI, the nearness to the river, and the great grey castle looming over the further bank. He used to say that Eton was unique among public schools in that, at least in his day, there was little bullying, beatings were not excessive, and boys were allowed very much to go their own way: it wasn't necessary to be a playing-field hero to be accepted by your fellows.

Under the headmastership, first of Edward Lyttelton, then of the Rev. Cyril Alington, Jack moved up through the school as a member of Henry Marten's house, which prided itself on an atmosphere of enlightened tolerance. At 13 when he first arrived at the school, my father was an appealing Lower Boy in his tail coat and striped trousers, with his pink cheeks, blue eyes and light brown hair, and I remember him once casually mentioning that at this stage he wasn't above earning the occasional sixpence in the well-established, time-honoured manner.

Jack's school reports give the impression of a modestly talented pupil, not backward, certainly, but showing little evidence, according to his tutors, of any particular talent or aptitude for hard work. In mathematics Lord Hastings's work was 'reasonably good, but he was not a prominent member of this division'; in English, 'diligent and painstaking … but on the whole he has not much gift of expressing himself'; only in history did he appear to rise above the mediocre: 'Lord Hastings [is] a boy of some ability in my opinion,'[5] Mr Headlam reported, 'ready to take a good deal of trouble when interested … His general appearance and demeanour, on the other hand, is lethargic.' As Jack moved up the school he made the house teams for cricket and football, undertook

---

[5] Geoffrey Headlam. With permission of the Provost and Fellows of Eton College.

the obligatory military training and joined the Debating Society, although there was no noticeable improvement in his academic achievement – 'more imaginative than able' was the consensus.

Significantly, however, his skill at remaining under cover, so well developed in adulthood, was already apparent. 'He is in most ways a normal type of boy of a rather thoughtful kind,'[6] wrote the headmaster, Edward Lyttelton. '[But] he rarely or never lets me know what he is thinking of till betrayed by an earth-shaking laugh.' This was a view endorsed by his housemaster, Henry Marten, in a report to Warner Huntingdon, in which Marten added that '[Hastings] remains a very nice, & pleasant person to deal with & one feels is very straight in the essentials of school life'.[7]

In the spring of 1916, when Jack had not yet been two years at Eton, the situation in Ireland, which had been growing increasingly tense, suddenly erupted with the outbreak of what became known as the Easter Rising. The Irish Republicans turned violently against their British rulers, heralding a period during which many Ascendancy properties were fired on, set alight, and otherwise destroyed. Jack, at home for the Easter holidays of 1916, was about to return to school when the situation exploded. 'It was a very frightening time,' he recalled.

One morning four armed men walked up the drive at Sharavogue and pounded on the front door. Fearing the worst, Warner himself came out to talk to them, but the men greeted him civilly and said they had no wish to harm anyone but he must hand over all guns immediately, a demand with which Warner unhesitatingly complied. Later the family realised how lucky they were not to have been murdered and the house burnt to the ground, how lucky that the local Irish loved hunting just a little more than they loathed the English. As Jack used to tell it,

---

[6] George Lyttelton to Henry Marten 1.3.17 idem.
[7] Henry Marten to Warner Huntingdon 5.3.17 idem.

'My father, having been a Master of Foxhounds, was in Irish eyes almost a sacred person'.

A couple of days later 15-year-old Jack, who with his sisters had spent part of the holiday cheerfully collecting Sinn Fein flags, set off on his journey back to school. His route took him through Dublin at the height of the crisis. The centre of the city was a war zone, with street battles between Republicans and the military, with rifle fire, exploding bombs, shops sandbagged, buildings aflame, trenches dug in St Stephen's Green, and Liberty Hall itself reduced to rubble by British artillery. In typically lackadaisical fashion, Jack on his arrival at Eton described this exciting experience to his father.

Dear Dada,

Thank you ever so much for my lovely holidays with the riding, fishing and shooting. I arrived quite safely in spite of the choppy crossing and lots of people were sick. It was very interesting seeing Dublin in ruins and I was lucky enough to go round with the King's messenger and saw everything. I picked up some war relics in Liberty Hall. I hope Mama, you, and everybody is quite well, also that Scamp is fit.

Yours affec.
Jack.

Maud herself was in England at the time, but so alarmed was she by the escalating violence that she began putting pressure on her husband to leave Sharavogue. Although it would be a wrench for Warner to abandon his family home, in recent years the Huntingdons had been spending several months of the year in England, renting a series of large country houses during the hunting season, with Warner in 1904 taking over as Master of the North Staffordshire, and in 1909 of the prestigious Atherstone hunt in Leicestershire. For Maud this new routine had been entirely beneficial, not least because it gave her easier access to

London where she could work on renewing and expanding her social contacts.

With three daughters to marry off, Maud's overriding purpose was to net them suitable husbands, not an easy task when so many promising young men had been killed or were otherwise occupied on the battlefields of northern Europe. From childhood the girls had been thoroughly drilled in etiquette by their mother. 'Never let a silence fall,' she would tell them, instructing them when at luncheon and dinner parties always to draw the man out first with a series of interested questions, only when necessary proffering some amusing anecdote of their own. In her own way Maud was fond of her children and believed she had their best interests at heart. 'You don't have to marry for money,' was a favourite saying, 'but always go where money is.'

Faithfully following this excellent maxim, she took each daughter in turn and launched her into the competitive maelstrom of the London season. Tightly corseted and expensively dressed, Kathleen, Norah and Marian were presented at court, photo-graphed for The *Tatler*, shown off at balls, at Ascot, Henley and Cowes, and on Saturdays to Mondays were escorted by their mother to aristocratic house parties the length and breadth of the British Isles. The three sisters accepted this intensive marketing without question: it was part of the natural order, what young women of their social class always did. Their own ambitions and personal preferences were largely irrelevant, although they each of them privately shared a strong desire to escape as soon as possible from their mother's dominion.

As was entirely proper, the eldest, Kathleen, was the first to be dispatched. Small, plump, bespectacled, Kathleen hardly appeared a promising proposition; she was lively and intelligent, however, and had inherited in full her mother's passion for the theatre. When only 16 Kathleen was taken by Maud to London for her first débutante season, and to everyone's surprise she immediately fell in love with a suitable young man with whom she quickly developed an understanding.

Unfortunately, before the engagement could be officially announced the press picked up on it, and Maud was so affronted by this breakdown in protocol that she immediately issued a denial and forced Kathleen to break off the relationship. Mutely obedient, Kathleen shortly afterwards was manoeuvred into a loveless match with a wealthy Leicestershire squire. William Curzon-Herrick, always known as 'Bunkie', was tall, fair, amiable and, according to Warner, 'fat as a boar pig'. He was also, in my father's words, 'backward, not quite like other boys'. Bunkie's passion was for railway timetables – he could recite the whole of *Bradshaw's* by heart – and, again according to my father, 'would have been happiest living life as a railway porter'. He did, however, have a great deal of money – 'inherited a cool million', Maud would tell people approvingly – and a fine house, Beaumanor, in the centre of the Leicestershire hunting country.

With Kathleen settled, Maud turned her attention to her younger daughters, Norah and Marian. It was to improve their chances of finding a husband that the two of them had been placed as ladies-in-waiting, or Maids of Honour, to the Vicereine, Lady Wimborne, at Dublin Castle. Alice Wimborne, with her beauty, charm and fabulously expensive wardrobe, played the role of Vicereine to the hilt, her impeccably regal bearing leading people to refer to her behind her back as 'Queen Alice'. Her husband, Ivor Guest, Lord Wimborne, was generally regarded as a bore and a bounder, pompous and far from intelligent ('We must assume that God knew best / When he created Ivor Guest ...' began a rude little rhyme that was in circulation before Guest succeeded to the title). But his wife, amusing and kind-hearted, was of a very different mettle, and all the Hastings family adored her. Behind her condescending public manner, Alice, with her dimples and golden eyes, was sexy and flirtatious, even with very young men such as my father, who remained besotted with her for years; later she was to have a long affair with the composer William Walton, 22 years her junior.

Maud and Alice Wimborne were old friends: when in London Maud frequently attended dinner parties at Wimborne House in Arlington Street, next to the Ritz; and on several occasions the two women collaborated in bazaars and the production of dramatic tableaux for fashionable causes. Thus Alice was delighted to take on Maud's girls as Maids of Honour when the Wimbornes were appointed to Dublin. The novelist and diarist Cynthia Asquith, who stayed at the Castle in 1916, gives a glimpse of Norah and Marian in their roles as ladies-in-waiting. 'We found Her Excellency and the Maids warbling at piano when we got back,'[8] wrote Lady Cynthia. 'After their Excellencies had withdrawn, the Maids of Honour … and I had a very blasphemous impromptu miracle play. We were all in Heaven – the sofa serving as "Abraham's Bosom". We really were very funny.'

Norah, the elder of the two 'Maids', was the next to be married. Gentle, artistic and rather dreamy, Norah was happiest leading a quiet life in the country surrounded by horses and dogs. Of the three sisters, she suffered most from her mother's relentless driving of her through a ceaseless round of dinners and balls. Like Kathleen before her, she had not been allowed to marry the man she loved, but fortunately her arranged match in 1920, for which Maud had ruthlessly schemed, developed into an amicable and long-lasting relationship. The Earl of Kilmorey, handsome and charming, owned an estate at the foot of the Mourne Mountains in what is now Northern Ireland, where he and Norah were to live for the rest of their lives.

Over time, however, the bruising effects of Maud's enforced socialising led Norah to flinch from most social contact, and in middle age to become a virtual recluse. Her husband eventually accepted that she should not be asked to entertain or, except on very rare occasions, to leave Mourne, while Norah for her part agreed to turn a blind eye to Kilmorey's activities on his frequent absences in London and elsewhere.

As it turned out, it was only the youngest sister who was to marry for love. Marian, lively, adventurous, affectionate and

---

[8] *Diaries 1915–1918*, Lady Cynthia Asquith (Hutchinson, 1968) p. 131.

very pretty, was far less tractable than Kathleen and Norah. She, like her sisters, had suffered under her mother's ruthless dictatorship, but unlike them she had taken matters into her own hands. At the age of 22, Marian had bravely defied her parents and married Patrick Cameron, a glamorous but impecunious young Captain in the Cameron Highlanders. Maud was so enraged by her daughter's disobedience that for several years she refused to see her or have anything to do with the young couple. '[Marian] had the ball at her feet,' Maud fulminated to Jack, '& might have married a really rich man of good family with plenty of this world's goods & had a delightful time, instead of having to *pig* it for the rest of her days among a lot of *middle class people*!' Marian for her part never regretted her decision, although she was understandably nervous in the early days of her great adventure. 'Oh Jack,' she wrote shortly after her wedding in July 1918,

> the parents will probably never see me again, but it was the only way, as they would not even listen to anything! ... You will see me some time, whatever Mama says Jack won't you – & do do write to me, it was so terrible going away all alone, & I do feel so lonely. Alice Wimborne saw us off at the station ... Do write very soon, – I think we will be awfully happy once things settle down a bit.

Jack, meanwhile, was coming to the end of his career at Eton. It may not have been a particularly distinguished career but at least he had made a number of lasting friendships. Before leaving in 1919, Jack's likely future was amicably predicted by a fellow member of his house: 'Jack Hastings will no doubt continue being delightfully lazy wherever he goes,'[9] the young man wrote, adding with curious prescience, 'and he may go out to Australia.'

The declaration of peace on 11 November 1918 had been marked at school by a half-holiday, fireworks, and in Marten's

---

[9] Marten's House 'Retrospect 1918.' With permission of the Provost and Fellows of Eton College.

House by a grand 'Sock Supper'. Toasts were drunk to His Majesty the King, to Marshal Foch, and a silent toast to those who had fallen in the war, the last a poignant reminder to Jack and his contemporaries that they were to be the first of their generation not to be sent to the front. In December Jack with other members of the Eton OTC passed into Sandhurst, preparatory to beginning full-time military training the following summer. In July, however, when the rest of his House left for camp at Tidworth, Jack was not among them: he had fallen ill with a sinus infection which became so severe that Maud, alarmed, decided to send him abroad to a warm climate for a couple of months.

For Jack this was a seminal experience. Accompanied by his Aunt Rowena ('Een'), one of Warner's sisters, he travelled abroad for the first time in his life, through France, to Italy, and then to the island of Capri. Brought up in Ireland in a house that was hung with pictures of horses, of hunting scenes, of packs of hounds and more horses, Italy came as a revelation and the beauty of Capri entranced him. Een, who was an enthusiastic amateur artist, bought Jack pencils, paper and a box of water-colours and he started to paint. 'It was so beautiful,' he said later, 'that there seemed only one thing to do.' Although he may not have realised it at the time, Jack had found his vocation, the direction which he was to follow throughout his life, and which was to set him on a very different path from that intended by his parents.

Completely recovered, Jack returned to England at the end of the summer, and in October 1919 went up to Christ Church, Oxford, to read History. Here again he was following in the footsteps not of his father but of his grandfather. Francis Huntingdon was no intellectual, but for the aristocracy of his time that was of little consequence: in those days there was no entrance examination, peers and sons of peers wore a gold tassel on their caps to distinguish them from lesser mortals, and in Christ Church it was customary for blue-blooded undergraduates to summon the college servants by a blast on the hunting horn. Admittedly much had changed since then, and from 1918 a more egalitarian period

had begun, with men returning from the war bringing a sophistication to university life that was impressive to boys just out of
school.

If Jack had been the Invisible Man at Eton, he left an even
fainter trail at Oxford, his name rarely appearing in either college
or university archives. Records show that at Christ Church he was
given a handsome set of rooms in Tom Quad, and studied under
the aegis of the history tutor, J. C. (later Sir John) Masterman. In
1921 he gained a commission as 2nd Lieutenant in the Territorial
Army having duly attended the University OTC, although he found
the weekly exercises – attending camp, taking part in parades
and sitting through lectures and demonstrations – unremittingly
tedious. True to family tradition, Jack paid greater attention to
recreation than to work, and indeed on the face of it might well
be categorised as one of those college hearties 'baying for broken
glass' so memorably described in *Brideshead Revisited* by another
member of that Oxford generation, Evelyn Waugh. Jack became
a member of the notorious Bullingdon Club, famed for the
arrogance and rowdy behaviour of its upper-class membership,
of the right-wing Carlton Club, and of Loder's, a drinking club
whose traditional toast was 'Long live the King and Foxhunting!'
He also hunted, attended point-to-points, and played polo for the
University, in 1922 scoring the only goal for his side in the annual
fixture against Cambridge.

Although barely out of his teens, Jack was also much in demand
for balls and parties in London. He was an attractive-looking
young man, tall, with blue eyes, a fresh complexion and light
brown hair. More importantly, he was an only son, a viscount and
heir to an earldom, and thus a prime target as husband material.
Ambitious mothers had him firmly in their sights, and during the
London season his mantelpiece was cluttered with invitations,
sometimes for as many as six or seven dances a night. Several
evenings a week he and others of his Christ Church set were on
the London train, known as 'the Flying Fornicator', returning
to Oxford in the small hours, hoping to avoid the university

police, the 'bulldogs', before climbing unsteadily over the wall into college.

Maud, of course, fully approved of her son's intensive social life, regarding his university career simply as an appropriate rite of passage. Despite Maud's substantial dowry, for some years the Huntingdons had been living beyond their means, and it was up to Jack not only to ensure an affluent style of living for himself but also, and as soon as possible, to restore the family fortunes. All Maud's hopes rested on her son, and she was determined to do everything in her power to find him a suitable wife. Objections on his part were brushed briskly aside. 'I know your argument about being too young,' Maud told him, '[but] young men had much better marry young if they can find the right girl … In life when you get a *really good* opportunity *take it* as you may never get it again.'

Maud's every available moment was now spent conspiring with other titled mothers, Lady Nunburnholme, Lady Strathmore, Lady Mar and Kelly, all of whom were firmly focused on promoting their children's prospects. A woman of ferocious energy and determination, this latter-day Lady Bracknell was not easily denied, and during the university vacations Jack was sent off on an almost ceaseless round of country-house parties, many of which he enjoyed: he loved hunting, was an excellent shot and adored dancing with pretty girls.

The social season of 1921 was the first to recover much of the luxury and glamour of the pre-war period. The great London town houses, Bridgewater House, Apsley House, Lansdowne House, were open again, and from May to July a series of sumptuous balls and parties were given whose extravagance gave little sign of the preceding years of shabbiness and deprivation. Night after night in Mayfair and St James's, canopies and red carpets appeared on the pavement as lines of chauffeur-driven motor cars drew up outside the brightly illuminated front doors. Inside, young women in chiffon gowns and with flowers in their hair were whirled round the magnificent ballroom by pink-cheeked young men, the girls carefully chaperoned by their mothers, who in diamond tiaras and perched on little gilt chairs watched beadily from the sidelines. At midnight, supper was served, with quantities of champagne, plovers' eggs and stuffed quail, smoked salmon and lobsters, meringues and ice-cream, to be followed two or three hours later by a big breakfast of bacon, eggs, sausages and cups of steaming coffee. Between four and five in the morning the band struck up God Save the King, overcoats and furs were collected, and the guests piled into their cars to be driven home to bed as dawn was breaking.

Jack was often a guest at these lavish entertainments, throughout the season his name appearing with some frequency in The *Tatler* and in the Court Circular of *The Times*. Viscount Hastings was one of the many titled guests at Lady Philipps's dance in Hill Street, Mayfair, where 'the ballroom was decorated with rambler roses, and the supper tables with malmaisons and sweet-peas';[10] he attended a dinner party of Lord Glentanar's, was a guest of the Wimbornes at Arlington House, at a party of Lady Belper's at the Embassy Club in Bond Street, and at a luncheon of Lady Cunard's in Grosvenor Square. He played polo at Hurlingham, one of the four members of the English team in their victorious match during the 'polo war' against the United States, and in August was on the Isle of Wight at the Royal Yacht Squadron for a party during Cowes Week.

By August the London season was over, the town houses closed up as their owners departed for the country or abroad for the rest of the summer. Grouse-shooting began on 4 August, and Jack, not his father's son for nothing, spent much of his time moving from one house party to another in Scotland and the north of England, his guns in their leather Purdey cases a crucial part of his luggage. From time to time my father would tell stories about these elaborately organised events, in almost every respect unchanged in format from pre-war Edwardian days: the tramping

---

[10] *The Times*, 27.6.23.

up and down hill over the heather, stalking deer; the long day out on the moor after grouse, followed by the welcome sight of a blazing fire and a large tea, with perhaps a game of bridge or mah-jongg before going upstairs to change for dinner; the formal dinners in the evening, and the, in his view, idiotic etiquette that forbad speaking to a girl to whom by oversight one had not been introduced.

On one occasion he was invited by the Strathmores to stay at Glamis Castle in Scotland. The Prince of Wales was of the party, clearly worshipped by the plump young daughter of the house, Lady Elizabeth Bowes-Lyon, who could hardly take her eyes off him. After dinner one evening, when the ladies had left the room and the men were sitting over their port, his equerry said to the Prince, 'Sir, I wish you would pay a little attention to Lady Elizabeth. She's very smitten by you.' 'Oh I can't,' replied His Royal Highness, languidly drawing on his cigar. 'She's too *fat*.'

Jack found much to enjoy in these house parties, and even as a very young man was well able to pull his weight as a guest. Rigorously schooled in good manners by his mother, Jack also had a gentle charm and a genuine interest in people that made him a likeable companion. For his part, he especially appreciated the company of attractive young married women, so much more sophisticated and flirtatious than the débutantes straight out of the schoolroom. One of his hostesses from Scotland, with whom he had spent some days fishing, wrote to him roguishly as 'Jackie, my dear & only love, my dear Rod-Mate', complaining that 'it seems so long since I saw, or heard, aught of you'. Then there was Mary Howe, the sister of Bunkie, Kathleen's husband, whom he first met at a shooting weekend at Beaumanor, 'one of the most beautiful women in England', as he described her, 'who had many fervent admirers'.

Clearly he counted himself among them, and often talked adoringly about her. From other evidence also, specifically the photographs and letters he chose to preserve, there are indications that with some of his hostesses he formed, or tried to form, more than a purely social acquaintance. The lovely Lady Belper, for instance, still only in her twenties, wrote to him after an evening at the Embassy Club:

> *Mon trés cher* Jack, I wonder if you are angry with me. I am not going to make excuses. I would, if we weren't friends, but, without any explanation, please believe that I never meant to hurt … If letters don't bore you, I shall inflict some on you from time to time just so that you will not forget me entirely … Please think nicely of me. Eva …

While perfectly ready to enjoy himself, however, Jack had no intention of submitting to his mother's plans, his recalcitrance in this context resulting in some furious letters from home. Maud had gone to considerable trouble to find suitable heiresses and yet each time she came up with a glittering new prospect, Jack – *stupid* boy! – had let her slip through his fingers. One promising young woman on whom Maud had set her sights was an American millionairess, a Miss Mellon, whom it was arranged Jack would drive to a dance in the country. Unfortunately the weather was bad, it never stopped raining, and suddenly in the middle of nowhere they had a puncture. Jack's incompetence at changing the tyre meant they missed the dance and Miss Mellon was so exasperated she told him she never wanted to see him again. Maud when she heard about it was intensely annoyed by her son's ineptitude, as she lost no time in telling him. 'They say *fortune* knocks at least *once* at every man's door. Any way *this* time you have missed it, & I can *never* as long as I live find you another such a charming beautiful girl with a fortune which will ensure every good thing the world can give to her & her husband.'

Maud was not one to give up easily, however, and it wasn't long before she had located a replacement, the beautiful, 18-year-old Donne Philipps, daughter of the shipping tycoon, Lord Kylsant. Yet, almost unbelievably, Jack wrecked his chances on this second occasion, too. His mother was furious. 'I must frankly own I'm *very disappointed*', she wrote to him.

Heiresses with *great* beauty & charm don't crop up every day, & are not to be had just for the picking up … I think Donne one of the *most charming* girls I have ever met & a very beautiful one *too* with a character just as good as she is lovely … You had a *very good* chance there as *both* the girl & her mother seemed to take a *great* fancy to you but by refusing their frequent invitations plainly showed you did not care about them.

As the lecture continued, Maud grew increasingly frank about her reasons for wanting Jack to marry well.

Remember that money with us is not plentiful, in fact it is *very short* & *even* if I get what I expect from Australia it will not make us *really well* off. We shall have to be *tremendously* careful & consider every penny, & if it falls through then we are done for & you may have to go & earn money as a *bank clerk* or something.

This letter was written in April 1921, when Jack was still in his first year at Oxford. The previous year the family had finally found a permanent base in England, in Leicestershire, which in previous centuries had been the Hastings's home county. Since 1916, when they had left Sharavogue, the Huntingdons had rented a series of country houses throughout the Midlands and it was a relief to Maud that she now had a fixed establishment from which to conduct a vigorous social life, while Warner, as Master of the Atherstone, was, as before, entirely taken up with the hunt.

Burton Hall was a sizeable, three-storeyed Georgian house of no great pretension to beauty. Surrounded by a small park, the house looked over a pleasant expanse at the back, with a wide terrace, a walled flower garden, a croquet lawn, and that fashionable feature of the Victorian age, a monkey puzzle tree; there were extensive stables at one side, and at the garden's outer edge was a ha-ha with an outlook beyond of flat fields, elm trees and grazing cattle. At the bottom of the drive there was the Home Farm and a small village, Burton-on-the-Wolds; there were several other farms on

the estate, leased to tenants, and a large area of woodland specifically reserved for pheasant-shooting.

Maud was glad to be settled in England, although she knew
there was little chance of persuading her husband to take part in
any social life in London. Her mother, Lady Wilson, had given up
her Mayfair town house and was now living on the south coast,
in Hove, so Maud rented a house in Manchester Square, where
she could entertain when she was in the capital. The fact that her
husband refused to join her there resulted in some painful disap-
pointments: Queen Mary, for instance, had declined an invitation
to a party of Maud's on the grounds that Lord Huntingdon would
not be present; and there was an extremely distressing occasion
when Maud was forced to forgo the opportunity of staying with
the Viceroy in India because Warner could not be persuaded to
undertake the journey.

None the less, Maud had been delighted by the move to England,
and when in Leicestershire she was pleased to find herself part of a
livelier and more fashionable society than she had had access to in
Ireland. At Burton her luncheon and dinner parties were meticulously planned, the menus varied and delicious, for although
Maud knew nothing about cookery she recognised instinctively
what was good about or wrong with any particular dish. She was
extremely fond of her food (invariably at Burton very rich) and
now in her fifties was growing stout, a couple of times a year
retiring to Harrogate or Baden-Baden in an attempt to lose weight.
Warner for his part was mostly indifferent to what was on his
plate, nor did he drink wine; instead he kept two kinds of whisky,
a fine Scotch for himself and his cronies, and what he referred to
as 'kill-dog whisky' which was offered to keepers and grooms.

Conveniently Burton lay halfway between the towns of
Loughborough and Melton Mowbray, Loughborough possessing
a theatre in the Town Hall ideal for amateur productions, while
Melton Mowbray, the 'Happy Valley' of the shires, was the sophisticated centre of the English hunting scene. Among the smart
set descending regularly on Melton was the Prince of Wales,

who took his hunting seriously and kept a permanent suite at the Craven Lodge Club, often accompanied by his brothers, the Dukes of York, Gloucester and Kent. During the season well-to-do Londoners, some of them only marginally interested in sport, came to stay at Melton, and evenings were crammed with cocktail and dinner parties and fancy-dress dances. All this was a great satisfaction to Maud, who was soon busily involved. In April 1922 she produced her first theatrical entertainment, in which Jack took part in a revue written by his sister Kathleen; the popular young conductor, Malcolm Sargent, who was based in Melton at the time, was roped in to oversee the show's musical content. Sargent quickly became a favourite of Maud's, regularly invited to Burton, where he made himself popular with the whole family. When he married the following year both Huntingdons were present at his wedding.

During the university vacations Jack made several trips abroad, to France and to ski in Switzerland, before returning to Burton, where he continued to hunt. This was his one real bond with his father, with whom in every other respect he felt he had little in common. And yet Warner was not unsympathetic: capable and intelligent, he had considerable charm, a quiet sense of humour and unfailing good manners, all of which made him much liked at all levels of society. The fact that his relations with his only son remained so distant remains something of a mystery.

Jack was always happier when staying with his sisters; with Kathleen – whose husband, Bunkie, had an excellent shoot at Beaumanor, only half an hour's drive away – and with Norah at Mourne Park in Northern Ireland. In January 1921 he was present at the christening of Norah's first child, he and Alice Wimborne among the godparents, and a year later he celebrated his 21st birthday at a dance given by Kathleen at Beaumanor. Of his youngest sister, Marian, to whom he was closest, he saw nothing as she had left England soon after her wedding. As though determined to move as far away from her parents as possible, Marian with her husband Patrick Cameron had sailed for the Falkland

Islands, where Patrick was to run a sheep station belonging to his family. Jack missed her presence sorely, but the two of them kept closely in touch, and although Jack's letters have of course disappeared, it is through Marian's correspondence that his movements can most usefully be tracked.

Jack had come down from Oxford in June 1922, leaving with an undistinguished third-class degree. No doubt galvanised by his mother's threat that he would end up as a bank clerk, he had decided to try for a career in diplomacy, writing to Harold Nicolson at the Foreign Office for advice. Nicolson sent a courteous reply and recommended a crammer in preparation for the notoriously challenging Foreign Office examination. Nothing came of this, presumably because Jack failed the exam, and in the event he was found a job with an old-established firm of stockbrokers, De Zoete & Gorton, in the City.

Before beginning on a career which held little attraction, Jack went to Germany for three months to learn the language. 'Dearest Jack,' Marian wrote to him from her remote outpost on the Falklands, 'I do envy you seeing Nuremburg & Heidelberg, they sound divine and I have always longed to see the blue Danube – is it very blue? And fancy champagne at 9d per bottle … It must be thrilling but rather sinister being all alone in a hostile country, do hope they won't knife you or anything … Well, I hope you don't lose your heart to a young fraulein …'

She herself was finding life in the southern hemisphere decidedly hard going, she told him, the terrain bleak, the climate wet, windy and bitterly cold. She also missed her brother ('I wish you could come out here & peer over the edge of the world with me'), and was concerned about his future. She knew he was more than capable of resisting 'the matrimonial wiles' of their powerful mother yet she worried that his indolent nature and habit of laissez-faire might lead him into a life of mediocrity and disappointment. 'Don't waste a day,' she encouraged him. 'I am sure it is better to do terrible things than to do nothing. Laziness in youth is a sin, how great one generally discovers – afterwards.'

Neither Marian nor anyone else could have foreseen how literally Jack was to follow his sister's counsel, and that the 'terrible things' that were about to take place would result in his departing for the other side of the world, drastically defying the traditions in which he had been brought up, and destroying for ever his relationship with his parents.

Such an upheaval could never have been predicted when in December 1923 Jack, after a morning at his office in the City, decided to walk to his club for lunch. On the way he ran into an acquaintance, a contemporary from school, who invited him to join a small group of friends lunching at the Savoy. Among them was a very lively, very striking Italian girl, Cristina Casati. She and Jack struck up an immediate rapport, and Cristina invited him to come with her on New Year's Eve to the Chelsea Arts Ball. It was during that evening, while dancing together at the Albert Hall, that their love affair began, an affair which was to have turbulent consequences, resulting in the two of them leaving England and embarking on a marriage that ultimately was to bring happiness to neither.

3

'Earl's Heir Weds Secretly'

My father's first wife, Cristina Casati, whom I never met, was rarely mentioned by either of my parents. When I grew old enough to think about it I at first assumed this was a matter of tact, that my father didn't wish to upset my mother by talking of her prede-cessor, that the subject of his earlier marriage might for her be a source of jealousy or resentment. In this I was wrong. On the few occasions when Cristina's name came up my mother remained equable, mildly interested, rather detached, while he seemed almost to blench, as if at the memory of some deeply damaging experience. Once or twice he made reference to Cristina's volcanic temper, the explosive scenes which for days afterwards left him feeling depressed and shaken, but this was never followed by any details of their life together. It was as though he had closed a door on that part of his emotional history, a door he was determined to keep shut. The strength of this determination occasionally became apparent, for instance at the time when my parents were on the point of buying a house in Gloucestershire: at the last minute they withdrew from the sale because my father discovered just in time that Cristina was living only a few miles away.

There must have been some continuing contact with the Casati family, however, because it was through my father that at the age of 18 I was given an introduction to them. This was some years after Cristina's death, and I had been sent to Rome for three months to learn Italian. A few days after my arrival I received a telephone message asking me to call the following afternoon on the Marchesa Casati at her apartment in the Palazzo Barberini. On reaching the massive and magnificent Palazzo, I walked through the tall iron gates flanked by palm trees, across the courtyard and, as instructed, into the lift to the first floor. Here the door was opened by a white-coated manservant who showed me into a vast, rather dark *salone* full of gilded furniture and enormous shadowy pictures. After a few minutes a tiny old lady came into the room. This was Anna, the second wife, and now widow, of Cristina's father. She was dressed in black, with a pearl necklace and earrings, her face, immaculately made up, was taut and deathly white, her fine hair dyed a pale blonde. She gently took my hand in both of hers and, looking up at me with a pair of enormous blue eyes, said in an unmistakably American drawl, 'I am so pleased to see you, *sono molto contenta di vederla, je suis trés contente de vous voir.*'

From that moment and until the end of my stay in Rome I became the Marchesa's pet, which made me feel very smug and cosseted. She would beckon me to sit next to her, stroking my hand as she talked; she spoke very softly, everything said in three languages, so conversation was often achingly slow. I saw her almost daily: I was present at her salon on Thursday afternoons, when she received members mainly of the old 'black' nobility – Colonna, Orsini, Borghese – while liveried footmen silently circulated the room proffering silver trays of sandwiches and little cakes; and I accompanied her, in her big, black, chauffeur-driven Buick, to dinners and bridge parties, to the trotting races at Tor di Valle, and once, to my slight consternation, to a private audience with the Pope. I met her son, Camillo, the Marchese, a courteous, slightly arrogant middle-aged gentleman with a passion for horses, and his luscious wife, Anna-Maria, an ex-chorus-girl from Naples. In those days, of course, there was no hint of the hideous scandal that was shortly to engulf Camillo and Anna-Maria, of group sex, suicide and multiple murder resulting in the almost total eradication of the Casati name from respectable Roman society. At that period Camillo was of interest to me only as the half-brother of Cristina, my father's first wife.

Cristina was the only child of an outstandingly ill-matched couple. Her father, Camillo, the Marchese Casati Stampa di

Soncino, was a member of an ancient Milanese family which, like the Huntingdons, had in recent times found its once considerable assets seriously depleted. In 1900 Camillo Casati, then in his early twenties, had married one of the richest women in Italy, Luisa von Amman, whose father had made a vast fortune in the cotton trade. By the time Luisa reached the age of 15 both her parents were dead, leaving her in possession of almost incalculable wealth, and in the eyes of the world it had seemed an ideal match, the traditional pairing of aristocrat with *nouvelle riche*, of the dashing, moustachioed young cavalry officer with the beautiful daughter of one of the country's great mercantile families.

It soon became clear, however, that the young people had little in common: Camillo, like Warner Huntingdon, cared only for hunting, which was of no interest whatever to his wife. Not long after their only child was born the Casatis agreed to live apart, Camillo moving to the Palazzo Barberini in Rome with a young American widow, Anna Cockerell, who eventually bore him a son. Cristina was only 13 when her parents separated, at which point she was made to decide between them. Not unnaturally, she chose to go with her mother.

Unfortunately for her daughter, Luisa Casati was wholly lacking in maternal instinct. Very shy as a child, Luisa since her marriage had transformed herself into one of the most extraordinary performance-artists of the age. Tall and extremely slender, she had turned herself into a surreal apparition, a living work of art: her thick tresses were red with henna, her face painted a ghostly white, her lips scarlet; her enormous dark eyes, the pupils enlarged with a daily dose of belladonna, were fringed with felt false eyelashes and lavishly rimmed with kohl. In Milan, Venice, Paris and Rome, the Marchesa Casati was famous for her outrageously ornate masked balls at which she would appear in costumes of a Byzantine magnificence, in dresses designed by Fortuny, Poiret and Bakst, loaded with jewels and often with a couple of snakes wreathed around her long arms.

The Marchesa was the first, possibly the only person for whom St Mark's Square in Venice was closed for a private party, at which she famously made her entrance accompanied by two diamond-collared cheetahs and a couple of naked boys covered in gold paint. Her portrait was painted again and again by, among others, Boldini, Van Dongen, Romaine Brooks and Augustus John; she was photographed by Beaton, de Meyer and Man Ray; sculpted by Troubetskoy and Epstein. Insanely extravagant and monumentally vain, Luisa craved admiration, and although little interested in personal relationships took a number of lovers, chief among them the poet Gabriele d'Annunzio, the 'Prince of Decadence', whose gift for self-dramatisation was almost equal to her own.

Deeply absorbed in her own baroque productions, Luisa had little time to spare for her daughter. Cristina's early years were spent first in Milan and then in Venice, in the magnificent Palazzo Venier dei Leoni on the Grand Canal. Here Luisa mounted her elaborately choreographed extravaganzas, maintaining a large retinue of servants as well as an exotic menagerie of birds, snakes, monkeys and big cats; she also had her own gondola, in which on more than one occasion her terrified small daughter was left alone with only the two cheetahs for company. Cristina was taught by a governess until the age of 11 when she was sent to a convent boarding-school in France where the girls were made to wear long cotton shifts while taking their baths.

During the holidays Cristina returned first to Venice, then later to Paris, where the Marchesa had taken another beautiful property, the Palais Rose, modelled on the Grand Trianon at Versailles and previously owned by Robert de Montesquiou, the model for that Proustian decadent, the Baron de Charlus. Yet, even while living under the same roof, Cristina saw little of her eccentric parent. Luisa was afraid that if she were known as a mother it would somehow seem 'ageing', so her daughter was kept very much in the background; until she was well into her teens Cristina was made to dress as a little girl, in white ankle socks and with her hair in bunches.

Cristina never felt close to either of her parents. Her father she barely knew, while there was nothing maternal about Luisa. Intensely narcissistic, she was nearly always on stage, rarely emerging from behind her heavily painted façade. In her extravagant costumes, the altitudinous high heels, the ropes of pearls, the top hats of tiger skin and black satin, she was a Commedia dell'Arte figure, to be applauded and extolled. Cristina admired her mother but was also daunted by her, too much in awe ever to feel any real affection.

In 1919, a year before Jack came up to Christ Church, Cristina was presented at Court, then sent to Oxford to perfect her English and to take courses as an external student at the university. At this period, the Marchesa came frequently to England to be with her most recent lover, the painter Augustus John; the two of them visited Oxford on several occasions, Augustus making a sketch of Cristina in which she looks both wary and sad. During her mother's absences Cristina's closest family connection was with Guglielmo Marconi, inventor of the radio telegraph. Marconi, an old friend of her father's, spent much of his time in England and was more than happy to keep an eye on Camillo Casati's daughter. A keen sailor, Marconi had rented a house near Southampton and during the summer Cristina was often a guest on his yacht, the *Elettra*, when Marconi would take her and his three children for days out on the Solent and in July to Cowes for the Regatta. After completing her studies Cristina moved to London, to a flat in Oxford Terrace (now Sussex Gardens) in Bayswater, and it was while she was living here, just before Christmas 1923, that she was introduced to Jack.

The two were almost exactly the same age, Cristina the younger by only six months, and the immediate attraction is not difficult to understand. Cristina, dramatic, passionate, outspoken, with an unerring sense of chic, was the antithesis of the nice English girls encountered on the débutante circuit; although not a beauty like her mother, her appearance was striking: she was tall and very slender, with a pale complexion, huge dark eyes and a sleek bob of chestnut-coloured hair. 'La marchesina Cristina Casati', an Italian paper admiringly reported, 'è alta, bruna, elegantissima ... e parla inglese perfettamente.' She was sportive, too, enjoyed swimming, was an accomplished horsewoman and enthusiastic dancer, known for her expertise at the tango.

Jack, for his part, tall and charming, was attractive to women, who responded to his susceptibility, to his obvious willingness to be amused and to a quiet strength of character unusual in such a young man. Despite the difference in their backgrounds and upbringing, he and Cristina soon discovered they had shared interests, in particular in painting and in travel; and inevitably in such a comparatively small society they had a number of friends in common. Cristina had been taken up by a group of upper-class bohemians, reckless and eccentric young people, fast-living and high-spending, determined to behave in a manner guaranteed to shock the older generation. For a young woman like Cristina, whose upbringing had accustomed her to unrelenting super- vision, such an unfettered society was intoxicating.

Among Cristina's most constant companions were those two well-known young men about town, Evan Morgan, heir to Viscount Tredegar, and Napier ('Naps'), Lord Alington, both wealthy, eccentric and predominantly homosexual. The pair had great appeal, were famously generous, courteous and kind- hearted, while at the same time capable of outrageously bad behaviour. At Tredegar, his family's magnificent seventeenth- century mansion in Wales, Evan lived riotously under the nose of his strait-laced father, entertaining extravagantly and pursuing a libidinous love-life among a wide range of members of his own sex. Naps Alington, his close friend and colleague in imaginative extravagance, was a talented dilettante currently involved in a tempestuous relationship with Tallulah Bankhead, the husky- voiced American actress whose scandalous conduct with both men and women was very nearly to result in her deportation.

Both Evan and Naps became fond of Cristina, and she stayed often at Tredegar and also at Crichel, the Alingtons' palatial eighteenth-century house in Dorset. Inevitably, however, it was her mother, the ultimate gay icon, who fascinated these two the most. When the Marchesa began appearing in England with Augustus John she was instantly taken up by Naps and Evan, both entranced by her extreme theatricality and obliviousness to common mundanity. Invited to stay for the first time at Tredegar she made the six-hour journey in a London taxi-cab, the enormous fare paid without comment by the butler who opened the door, while Naps was so taken with Luisa that he bought one of the two portraits John painted as well as a bust by Epstein.

Cristina had no wish to compete with her mother, in whose presence she was noticeably subdued, nor did she indulge in the wild hedonism of Naps and Evan. She enjoyed their company, however, and was often present at their large, frequently chaotic house parties, most often at Crichel, as Naps's sister, the lovely and 'remarkably wanton' Lois Sturt, was Cristina's closest friend and confidante. The two young women shared an interest in clothes and in painting – Lois had studied art and had her own studio in Chelsea – and also in the theatre, although Cristina, unlike Lois, had no desire herself to go on stage. Lois was deeply immersed in a secret affair with the married and much older Earl of Pembroke, 'Reggie', while Cristina before she met Jack was for a time in love with Colin Campbell, brother of the heir to the Duke of Argyll. While at Crichel, the two young women spent long afternoons lounging about the drawing-room, smoking, listening to the gramophone and talking about their men and what they wanted to do with the rest of their lives.

When they were in London Cristina and Lois mixed with a small group of actors and upper-class bohemians; their set included Tallulah Bankhead, obsessively in love with Naps, Tony Gandarillas, the fashionable, party-going Chilean diplomat, the beautiful American heiress Alice Astor, banker's daughter Poppy Baring, and Teddie Gerard, music-hall star and mistress of the retail magnate, Gordon Selfridge. With the post-war dance craze at its height, most evenings were spent in nightclubs, from the

Embassy in Bond Street patronised by the Prince of Wales, to the far less respectable Cave of Harmony, the Blue Lantern and Mrs Meyrick's notorious '43', which was regularly raided by the police. Sexually liberated, both men and women drank heavily and quite a few took morphine and cocaine.

For her part Cristina, vivacious and excitable, adored dancing, but her behaviour never went to the extremes of some of her companions; she never took drugs nor drank to excess, and her eccentricities went little further than playing the ukulele and keeping a pet snake in her bedroom. And unlike most of her young women friends, Cristina's finances were not limitless and she frequently found herself in debt. Her mother provided her with a generous allowance but with no guidance whatever on how to stay within it. Cristina, innately elegant, liked to dress well and was frequently spending far more than she could afford on couture dresses, on hats, shoes and furs, with the result that she was forced to supplement her income by giving Italian lessons and on more than one occasion pawning her jewellery.

At the time Cristina met Jack, at lunch at the Savoy in December 1923, her affair with Colin Campbell was over and she was beginning to feel somewhat aimless and adrift. Jack was also far from happy: he found intolerable the constant pressure from his mother to marry him off and he was growing daily more convinced that a career as a stockbroker was not for him. During the week he lived at 1, Manchester Square, a fine five-storey Georgian house, fully staffed, which Maud used as her London base, and which he shared with Geoffrey Gibbs, a friend from Eton. From here every morning, in dark suit, with briefcase, bowler hat and newly grown moustache, he commuted to Throgmorton Street, but the longer he worked there the more intensely he grew to dislike it. Working in the City, he said, was like living in a sewer and he could hardly wait to make his escape.

Fortunately Jack had access to an unusually interesting social life, which provided a welcome antidote to the tedious hours immured in his office. Although still in his early twenties, he had a wide circle of acquaintances, not only from school and university but among an older generation, many of them encountered through those two formidable hostesses, the Ladies Wimborne and Cunard. It was by Alice Wimborne, for instance, that Jack was introduced to Osbert Sitwell, who subsequently invited him on a number of occasions to his house in Carlyle Square. In later life Jack would describe those soirées which clearly made a great impression: the eccentric décor of greeny-gold wallpaper, the mother-of-pearl, the conch-shaped chairs and dolphin tables, the sea shells, wax flowers, and the eclectic collection of paintings by Picasso, Modigliani, Sickert, Gertler and Paul Nash. Here while drinking strong cocktails and in a cloud of cigarette smoke Jack talked and listened to the young composers, William Walton and Constant Lambert, to Arnold Bennett, Walter Sickert, Lytton Strachey and Percy Wyndham Lewis.

Jack was a frequent guest, too, at the notoriously intimidating luncheon parties of Emerald Cunard, where the hostess would suddenly signal for silence with a tap on her glass before pointing to her victim – 'Jack, dear, will you explain to us about Art?' It was here that Jack met the Armenian novelist and man about town, Michael Arlen – 'the only Armenian not to have been massacred', as Emerald somewhat tactlessly introduced him – who was shortly to become both rich and famous with the publication of his novel, *The Green Hat*. He and Jack took to each other at once; 'a very gay and pleasant companion', as Jack described him. The two of them stayed often with Jack's sister Kathleen at Beaumanor, where Arlen worked on his novel while simultaneously pursuing an affair with Kathleen's sister-in-law, the beautiful Mary Howe.

As always, Jack kept in close touch with his sisters, and he made regular duty visits to Burton to see his parents. Both Huntingdons believed they were doing their best by their son: he was provided with free accommodation in London; his father paid his tailors' bills, his club memberships and even gave him a car, which, never a skilful driver, Jack wrote off almost at once. Although apparently unable to express it there is no doubt Warner felt concern for

Jack, worried that he seemed to be falling under the influence of some highly dubious characters. Since his time at Oxford Jack had known both Naps Alington and Evan Morgan, neither of whom were models of propriety; nor was another member of their group, 'Boy' Torby, son of Grand Duke Michael of Russia, a talented amateur painter whose fondness for recreational drugs deeply shocked the older generation.

'Whatever you do leave drugs alone or you will be like young Torby', Warner wrote to Jack after some particularly depraved behaviour was reported to him. Most worrying of all, in his father's view, was Jack's association with Gavin Henderson, another ex-Eton and Christ Church contemporary. Gavin, heir to Lord Faringdon and 'a roaring pansy', as one contemporary described him, had, like Jack, a powerful mother, a friend of Maud's, who eventually succeeded in bullying him into marriage. In hysterical reaction Gavin organised a riotous stag night during which, with 20 gallons of petrol from a local garage, he literally set the Thames on fire, while next day at his fashionable wedding he outraged respectable society by inviting the black singer Florence Mills with her supporting cast of Blackbirds, celebrating his wedding night with a sailor picked up earlier in the evening. Underneath this flamboyant behaviour, however, Gavin was intelligent and astute, his youthful rebelliousness later translating into a political idealism of the far left very similar to Jack's; their alliance endured, with Gavin remaining for Jack a patron, colleague and lifelong friend.

Jack's affair with Cristina, which properly began at the Chelsea Arts' ball, continued at full intensity during the early months of 1924. The two of them met whenever they could, in London and also in various safe houses in the country, primarily at Crichel and Tredegar as both Naps and Evan were extremely supportive, as were Lois Sturt and Reggie Pembroke, who had their own illicit relationship to keep hidden. From long experience Jack knew it was essential to keep the affair secret from his mother, and to this end he and Cristina were careful to avoid appearing together at social events where their presence might be reported to Burton. Cristina's parents, on the other hand, presented less of a threat, neither of them appearing greatly concerned about their daughter's companions or way of life; and from their point of view young Viscount Hastings must have seemed eminently suitable as an escort.

Jack met Luisa on several occasions, both fascinated and appalled by her vanity and eccentricity, while she seems hardly to have noticed him, just another of her daughter's friends. The Marchese, on the other hand, rather took to Jack: Camillo Casati, Master of the Rome Foxhounds and a keen polo player, regularly came over to England to hunt and was a judge at the International Horse Show at Olympia. Why should he not approve of a young man whose interests seemed so similar to his own?

Jack and Cristina, meanwhile, continued to see each other as often as possible, during the week dining and dancing at various restaurants and nightclubs. One of their favourite haunts was the Cavendish Hotel in Jermyn Street, whose eccentric proprietor, Rosa Lewis, was immortalised by Evelyn Waugh in his novel, *Vile Bodies*. The clientele of the Cavendish was divided between respectable couples up from the shires and some extremely louche but well-born young men whom Rosa treated with an almost maternal indulgence: Evan Tredegar was one, for instance, who kept a permanent suite at the Cavendish where he knew a blind eye would be turned to his far from respectable companions.

Jack, too, was always welcomed by Rosa, largely because Maud, half unwittingly, had come to her rescue during a court case: an American family had refused to pay because of the intolerable racket that had continued throughout the night. Maud, who was by this stage slightly deaf, had slept in a room on the same corridor and declared truthfully that she had heard nothing, testament which resulted in Rosa winning her case. Thereafter Rosa always referred to Maud as 'my mascot' and made a point of extending a special welcome to the Hastings family, and to Jack in particular.

Determined to keep their relationship as private as possible, inevitably Jack and Cristina were often apart, and during these periods of separation Cristina wrote Jack long yearning letters, telling him how deeply she loved him and how passionately she longed for their next meeting. 'Lois & Reggie have been extraordinarily kind to me & done there best to make me laugh again [but] I do miss you so much,' she told him after a weekend with Jack at Crichel.

> Even not seeing you all the time, but knowing you were in the house made such a difference. I wonder all the time if you still go on loving me … I'm longing, longing to see you my own darlingest pink Face. Please wire if I can see you. I get so thrilled every time I think of you & that is so often. Those blue eyes with a great big black centre. Oh! darling I do so want to have you near me.

Inevitably Jack's side of the correspondence has not survived, but at this stage he was clearly infatuated. Cristina was so different from most of the English girls he knew, lively, sexy and eccentric, full of vitality and enthusiasm. It was this 'marvellous enthusiasm' that was most remarked upon: 'your enthusiasm for everything is so contagious,'[11] one friend wrote admiringly, '& you know better than anyone I have ever met how to get the most out of things'.

Cristina was always able to spark Jack into action when, as often happened, he relapsed into what his sister Norah referred to as his 'lethargic groove'. There were occasional quarrels, of course, as Cristina was hot-tempered and quick to take offence, but in her frequently misspelt letters she was prompt to apologise and eager to make up. 'Darling, I know its all my stupid fault but that dosent make it better … What I wold really like is for you to be here … & talk about all the things that bother us & that might put a cloud between us.'

At this stage, however, the contretemps were few and easily forgotten in the strength of their mutual attraction, and there was

---

[11] Clifford Wight to Cristina Hastings 12.12.32. HRC.

an important bond, too, in their difficult childhoods, Cristina with her insanely self-centred mother and Jack with the domineering Maud. The Marchesa, who had recently taken off on a grand tour through Europe and the United States, may not have been unduly concerned about her daughter's future but Jack knew Maud was still concentrating all her efforts on finding him a suitable wife, and if she got wind of his affair with Cristina the reaction would be explosive.

Then at the beginning of 1925 Jack suddenly threw up his job and went abroad. It is not clear exactly what happened but by early March Jack was in Italy at the start of an absence of nearly three months. As before, when at the age of 18 he was taken to Capri by his Aunt Een, so now the main purpose of the trip was to paint. His seriousness about painting was wholeheartedly supported by Cristina who, if on a rather more modest scale, had artistic aspirations of her own. 'Your mentioning the arts started me too', she wrote to him. 'I've been reading pirat stories & illustrating them ... Oh! I'm going to try & do Lyno cutts, same as wood cutts but its on lenolium instead. Hedious, but great fun.'

During the weeks he was away Cristina wrote almost daily, keeping him up to date with what she was doing – 'I've been rushing round like a Catherine wheel ... Naps arrived Monday & we have had some really good parties' – and plaintively longing for his return. 'Darling, Its so dreadful to think that you are going farther & farther away from me', she wrote. 'Such a lot of sea and land between us ... Spero che non mi hai dimenticato completamente[12] ... You are the centre of all my emotions & they are rather painful now you are such a long way away from me ... penso a te tutto il tempo[13] ... I feel like as if something was drawing my heart & soul towords you. The strain hurts.'

Jack meanwhile was moving from Rome to Naples, Capri and finally to Sicily. It was in Palermo that he was reunited with

---

[12] 'I hope you haven't completely forgotten me'.
[13] 'I think of you all the time'.

his sister Marian, who with her husband Patrick Cameron had recently returned to Europe on leave from the Falklands. The three of them stayed at the same hotel, the romantic Villa Igeia, joined there by Alice Wimborne, who six years previously had so fondly waved Marian away on her honeymoon. Diligently Jack reported his movements to Cristina but his letters were disappointingly brief and unemotional, his reluctance ever to put pen to paper a source to her of frequent frustration. Now, in between the expressions of love and yearning, there began to appear with increasing regularity what were to become familiar complaints from Cristina about the inadequacy of Jack's correspondence. 'I haven't heard from you for days. Is your great art so filling your life? … I think you might have writen your Crissy a line even if only on a *postcard*. Have you compleatly forgotten me?'

As bad luck would have it, a few weeks before Jack was due to return, Cristina was deputed to drive her mother in the Marchesa's Hispano-Suiza to Spain. 'This is really the saddest thing that's ever hapend', Cristina complained. 'Darling Darling I do want to see you so terribly badly. You've been away so long it seems ages Uff Uff … I'll just ruch through countrys as quick as possible to be back very soon … I'm so afraid you will have changed when I get back. I love you very (lots & lots of verys) much.'

Then, shortly after her return, Cristina fell ill and was moved into a nursing home in St John's Wood, after which, accompanied by Naps Alington, she went to Switzerland to convalesce. Here she soon revived in the mountain air. 'Crissy is feeling *well!*' she reported to Jack. 'Let me know a short time before you return so I can let my nalis grow in your honour … I'm longing to see my pink face with lots of the whitest of teeth. Do you still look the same please don't change.' Jack returned to England in May 1925, but if Cristina believed he was now ready to settle down she must have been dismayed when she learned of his plan to leave again almost immediately.

One of the friendships Jack had made while at university was with an American postgraduate, William McGovern. A glamorous

figure, tall, handsome, clever and amusing, McGovern spoke 12
languages, and had been educated in Japan, France and Germany
before arriving at Christ Church. Although four years older than
Jack, the two had formed a firm alliance, and Jack was both envious
and impressed when McGovern on leaving Oxford had set off on
his first expedition, to the then unexplored kingdom of Tibet. On
his return McGovern wrote a best-selling account of his adventure,
To Lhasa in Disguise (later the inspiration for the film series about
Indiana Jones), which Jack read and found enthralling, leading
him to suggest that the two of them should mount an expedition
together. 'I was attempting to settle down & lead a humdrum &
more or less respectable existence in London,' McGovern recalled,
'when an old college friend, Viscount Hastings, looked me up, and
announced he was planning an Amazon-Andes expedition. He
asked me to be the co-leader of the new undertaking.' The ill-fated
Col. Fawcett had recently left for South America to search for the
lost city of El Dorado, and the jungles of Brazil were much in the
news. Inspired by Fawcett's example, Jack suggested that he and
McGovern should make a plan to explore the upper reaches of
the Amazon. The expedition would be expensive, but McGovern
succeeded in striking a remunerative deal with the *Daily Express*,
while Jack to his surprise won a promise of financial backing from
his father.

It is likely that Warner's offer was inspired by a genuine
sympathy for his son and for his spirit of adventure, but also by an
increasing disquiet about his unsettled way of life. When Jack gave
up his job in the City there was a period of worried consultation
between his parents, both afraid that he might now drift into
some wholly unsuitable occupation. At this stage neither of the
Huntingdons knew much about Cristina, but both were growing
increasingly anxious about Jack's failure to take his responsibilities
seriously, in terms either of finding a wife or of making a solid
career for himself.

It was Maud who now came up with the idea of sending him out
to Australia: through her father, she owned a substantial interest

in a sheep station in New South Wales, and it would be easy for Jack to find work there for a few months, which would not only keep him out of trouble but provide him with some valuable experience. Meanwhile Warner's offer partly to finance the South American expedition could thus have been a form of bribe: if Jack were allowed one final chance to sow his wild oats, then surely on his return from Australia he would be prepared to conform, to marry and play his part as a dutiful member of the family, a son and heir of whom his parents could at last be proud.

It was at this point, with Jack deep in discussion with McGovern over plans for South America, that the Huntingdons were tipped off about his affair with Cristina. The news appalled them: the very idea that their son should have taken up with this notoriously fast young woman, a *foreigner*, even worse a Roman Catholic, was outrageous! Immediately Maud fired off a couple of furious letters to Jack about Cristina's shocking behaviour, her scandalously immoral mother, and her group of disgustingly decadent friends. The Marchesa Casati, Maud was reliably informed, 'is an *impossible* person & is not only *immoral* but *absolutely unmoral* & her reputation is in every way of the very *worst*. She always hated her child & only wanted to get her out of the way & that is the reason she was so badly brought up & has learned no manners.'

As to Cristina's friends, Lois Sturt was the centre of a 'vicious circle of uncivil little actresses', while everyone agreed that 'Tallulah Bankhead is considered one of the most heinous & *depraved* women in London'. This barrage was followed by a letter from Warner, no doubt written at his wife's instigation, in which he forbad Jack ever to see Cristina again, threatening if he disobeyed to cut him off with the traditional shilling. Jack's immediate reaction was twofold: to propose to Cristina and to cancel his plans for the expedition. 'We were busy making final preparations for departure,' wrote McGovern, 'when urgent family matters suddenly forced Lord Hastings to stay in England, & I was left with the sole burden of the expedition on my shoulders.'

When telling the story in later life, my father rather ungallantly used to say that as far as he was concerned the affair with Cristina was coming to an end. Over the past year it had become increasingly apparent that the relationship was unequally balanced: Cristina was deeply in love with Jack, but although he had been infatuated for a while and remained very fond of her, he was not in love, and was certainly not interested in marriage. Most significantly, he had come to dread her explosions of temper, the 'scene nere' ('black scenes'), which erupted with increasing frequency: even a minor annoyance, it seemed, could set her off, and she would scream and rant hysterically, leaving him shaken and depressed for days while she, apparently unaffected, recovered within minutes. After suffering from his mother's temper in childhood he found Cristina's rages unbearable, and it was mainly for this reason that he would frequently disappear, leaving her unhappy and penitent, imploring him to return. Indeed it is entirely possible that his three months in Italy, and his plans for an expedition to Brazil, were partly motivated by a desire to distance himself from Cristina.

Warner's letter changed everything, and from that moment events moved fast. Jack and Cristina were now constantly together, planning their future. If for rather different reasons, both saw in the uproar their opportunity for escape. They agreed it would be impossible to stay in England and as Jack had been due shortly to sail to Australia, it was a simple matter to convert his ticket from first class to second. Most of their own friends were supportive, in particular Lois and Naps, who at Crichel provided a refuge where the couple were always welcome to recuperate for a few days from the hectic activity in London and the bombardment of letters from Maud.

Finally, without a word to any member of his family, Jack obtained a special licence for a civil ceremony to be conducted on 21 October 1925 at the registry office of St George's, Hanover Square. In the hope of avoiding attention, he had made no mention of his title, giving his name simply as Francis John Hastings, but still the press got hold of it. 'Earl's Heir Weds Secretly', the headlines announced. 'With great secrecy,' the *Evening News* reported, 'the wedding took place in London yesterday of Viscount Hastings, son and heir of the Earl of Huntingdon, and Miss Cristina Casati, a beautiful girl, well known in artistic circles and a clever exponent of the tango.' 'The Earl and Countess knew nothing whatever about the wedding', gloated the *Daily Chronicle*, 'and the news of the marriage caused astonishment in the entire household.' Only *The Times* confined itself to the barest statement of fact – 'The marriage took place quietly yesterday morning ...'[14] – until four days later when the following sentence appeared in the Court Circular: 'We are authorised to state the marriage contracted by Viscount Hastings and Miss Casati last week at a registry office in London was without the consent, approval, or knowledge of his parents or family.'

And so it had been. Neither Maud nor Warner nor even Jack's sisters had had any inkling of what he intended to do, and the shocking news was communicated only by chance. Early on the morning of the 21st someone, possibly a journalist, had telephoned Maud at Burton asking what time the ceremony was due to begin. Astonished, Maud immediately put a call through to the house in Manchester Square to speak to Jack. The manservant who answered informed her that he had just been up to his lordship's room to call him as usual and found to his surprise the bed had not been slept in. By the time full realisation dawned, the wedding had taken place and there was nothing to be done. Unlike the Huntingdons, Cristina's mother in Paris had received some warning, her daughter having sent her a cable 24 hours in advance. The Marchesa made no objection: she was about to appear at a fancy-dress ball at which the train of her complicated costume was to be carried by eight gilded dwarves, and understandably she had little time to worry about other matters.

The brief ceremony was conducted during the morning, the couple accompanied to the registry office by a small group of

---

[14] *The Times*, 17.10.25.

friends, Naps Alington and Guglielmo Marconi, who acted as witnesses, as well as Lois, her lover Reggie Pembroke, Tony Gandarillas and Poppy Baring. The wedding itself took only ten minutes, after which the party returned to Ebury Street for lunch, remaining there till nearly six o'clock when the newly married pair, accompanied by Poppy and Naps, left by car for Dover where they spent the night. While at Dover Jack was cornered by a journalist to whom he gave as tactful an account of recent events as he could. 'We had no intention of keeping the wedding secret,' he claimed. 'The secrecy was the result of the fact that the ceremony had to be hurried on account of a business trip. If we had had more time at our disposal matters would have been arranged differently, although I do not like ceremony very much.'

The next morning Jack and Cristina drove the few miles to Folkestone where they caught the ferry to Boulogne, and from there motored down to the south of France, joining their ship, RMS *Ormonde*, at Toulon. As they went on board a handful of congratulatory telegrams were handed to them, from Lois, from Marconi, and from a friend of Jack's, Francis Stonor. 'I have just heard of your marriage to Christina!' wrote Stonor. 'If there is anyone in the world who deserves happiness, it is yourself, because you have the rarest of all gifts, of causing it in other people.'

But there were other communications that had also come on board at Toulon, and these were far from congratulatory. Maud, beside herself with rage at the news of her son's clandestine marriage, had immediately written to her contacts in Australia instructing them to give no help, indeed to have nothing to do with her delinquent son, who as a consequence of his deceitful and treacherous behaviour was no longer recognised as a member of the family. These letters she entrusted to an old friend, 'Hoppy' Howard, who by chance was also sailing on the *Ormonde*. During his first evening on board, Jack ran into Hoppy Howard in the bar. Delighted to see him, he offered to buy him a drink, and during the course of their conversation Hoppy disclosed what was in his luggage. In fact he had the letters with him this very moment, said Hoppy, right here in this briefcase, and putting the case on the table between them he excused himself to go and change for dinner. As soon as he had gone Jack opened the case, took out the pile of envelopes addressed in his mother's hand, and threw them overboard. Neither he nor Hoppy referred to the matter again.

Except for a small tropical storm as the ship approached Colombo, the weather during the voyage was calm, with only the usual shipboard activities – deck quoits, cinema shows, lectures, a couple of fancy-dress parties – to break the monotony of five weeks at sea. Among the passengers were a number of returning Australians and several British grandees, including an old acquaintance of the Hastings family, Lieut.-General Sir Tom Bridges, Governor of South Australia, with his wife and daughter. After the tumult of the preceding weeks, Jack and Cristina might well have been glad of this period of inactivity, grateful for the opportunity to relax and to enjoy each other's company without fear of reprisal. And yet this was far from the impression that was eventually conveyed: as bad luck would have it there was more than one acquaintance of Maud's among the passengers who took the trouble to send some highly coloured observations back to Burton.

'[Cristina's] behaviour on the boat was too awful for words', it appeared. 'Always in the bar till all hours in the night, drinking & laughing & shrieking while her husband would be left alone – this on their honeymoon. *Everybody* was horrified.' No one, of course, was more horrified than Maud. 'I am sorry to say that I have learned from 3 different sources of the way your wife behaved in the ship going out', she wrote to Jack. 'It was simply a *scandal*. They all say she laughed & talked so loud you could hear her voice all over the boat & rolled her eyes & flirted with every male on board & you were left by yourself & neglected. English ladies, or in fact any well bred women, don't do such things. It is vulgar & bad form.'

When the *Ormonde* docked in Melbourne on 25 November a group of reporters was waiting on Prince's Pier, eager for details of the widely reported 'secret marriage'. Yet again, Jack felt obliged to deny all reports of friction between himself and his family. 'An emphatic contradiction was given yesterday by Viscount Hastings … to statements which have appeared in a section of the Australian press regarding his marriage', reported the Melbourne *Argus*. 'Phrases such as "secret marriage" and "lightning romance" have appeared persistently', he remarked. 'They are absolutely misleading and rather annoying. I was engaged to my wife for a considerable time, and my family were perfectly aware of it … There was no "secret wedding" at all.' With that, Jack in trilby and dark suit, Cristina in a smart hat and coat, climbed into a waiting taxi and drove off to their modest hotel.

4

'Are sheep more interesting than they look?'

It was only a matter of days after Jack and Cristina docked in Melbourne that letters began arriving from England. One of the first was from Jack's sister Norah.

> *Well! Well!! Well!!! Well!!!!!!* [Norah began] So you decided after all to take the plunge – I will first of all be frank, for what is true friendship without frankness? – & say that I am *dreadfully* sorry in a way you had to do it *the way* you did it … as it gave the parents such a lever in the money line, & of course needless to tell you in the things they said – of you both –! … Dada was *terribly* upset & Mama of course just *boiled*.

On reflection, however, she agreed that elopement must have seemed the only practicable way of escape. 'I expect there were a million "wheels within wheels" working which made it impossible for you to take any other course, and I *know* what Mama is, & to understand that "c'est tout pardoner"!!' Norah ended her long letter by wishing the newly married pair the best of luck 'in that land of hearty colonials … It will be the devil of a fight if you have no money but I hope you will both be frightfully happy. As you say, you will certainly need courage.'

Like Norah, the other sisters, too, strongly supported Jack, although Kathleen admitted she had been appalled when she first heard the news. Marian, however, was wholeheartedly delighted, immediately sending a cheery letter from the Falklands. 'It is very difficult to write, as I don't know whether I'm writing to a cowboy riding the range or gold digging or whatever one does in Australia

… [but] all best wishes & congratulations. I hope you'll both be terribly happy, though I can hardly take in the idea of you as a married man, it seems absurd.' What about wedding presents, she went on to ask in the same light-hearted tone. 'Would Cristina like a seal, & you a penguin, or would you rather have a Postal Order?'

This was very different in tone from the letter Jack now received from his mother. Maud had had such high hopes, and now everything had been ruined by his disastrous marriage to this frightful foreigner. Not only had he bitterly disappointed his parents and ensured for himself a miserable marital future, but he had wrecked any chance he might have had to make a prosperous career in Australia, as she lost no time in telling him. 'If you had gone out as a *bachelor* … [or] married a sweet young English girl things would have been *so different*. *Every* door would have been open to you & you could undoubtedly have got a good staff *appointment* in any Government House. But making this odd secret marriage has spoilt everything.'

No words, of course, were too bad for Cristina, and it was imperative that Jack be made to realise the true nature of the woman who was now his wife. 'You have been made a *mug*, Jack … I'm afraid your wife will be no help to your career, & will spend *all* your money … You have married a girl with no *bringing up*, who has simply run wild. She is like an *unbroken in* filly. *You* must either break her in or she will *break you*.' The forthright criticism of Cristina continued. 'She has bad manners & no charm & does not *go down* with people & her appearance is so odd. Must she dye her hair that *dreadful* colour, *no one* peroxides their hair nowadays. Even if people have no looks they can be natural-looking & pleasant.' And if all that were not bad enough there was the sinister threat implicit in Cristina's Catholicism, anathema to any decent member of the Church of England. '*Don't* be coaxed into the Church of Rome, Jack. You would be under the forces of the priests who will take all your money & if your wife misbehaves herself you couldn't divorce her … Personally I foresee the end of your marriage will only be a matter of time.'

In contrast to these angry outpourings was the letter Jack received from his father. Warner Huntingdon had also been deeply wounded by his son's defection: his wife reported him looking 'very sad & depressed', while Norah in her letter had described their grieving father as 'a pathetic object'. Typically, however, there was little expression of such emotions in the brief communication which Jack received soon after his arrival in Australia. 'My dear Jack,' wrote Warner,

> I cannot let Xmas pass without sending you a line as it comes so far above earthly troubles. You are probably having better weather than we are here with frost & fog & no hunting owing to foot & mouth disease. I don't know what you have done about your clubs but if you wish I will write & ask for your name to be put on the list of members gone abroad. Wishing you good health & a comfortable Xmas, Your affec. Dada

In Melbourne, meanwhile, in the unaccustomed heat of the Australian summer, Jack and Cristina were taking stock of their situation and trying to work out what they should do. On their arrival there had been a flurry of excited reports in the press: the story of the runaway marriage had been widely circulated and the gossip columns were full of sightings of Viscount Hastings, 'one of the most utterly utter aristocrats who have ever visited these shores',[15] and of his glamorous wife, 'herself the daughter of a "dinkum" Italian marquis'. It had not gone unnoticed, either, that unlike other arriving grandees the couple were not met off the ship by a member of the viceregal staff, nor had they called at Government House, and, most eccentrically, they had chosen to stay not in one of the city's big hotels but in a small flat next to a roller-skating rink on St Kilda Road.

For Jack his immediate prospects were clear: long before his parents learned anything about Cristina, it had been arranged that he should go to work on the family sheep station in New South

---

[15] *The Truth*, 15.5.26. Melbourne.

Wales, a large share in which had been inherited by Maud from her father. For several months letters had been passing between Maud at Burton and the Wilsons' lawyers in Melbourne in preparation for the arrival of the son and heir. Thus, Jack knew what to do but Cristina did not, and with money so short she could hardly afford to be idle. Fortunately, a job was secured almost at once: her height, slender figure and Italian chic having been much remarked upon, she was offered the position of house-model at Georgette's, a fashionable dress-shop on Collins Street, the most prestigious shopping street in the city. The announcement of the news caused quite a flutter. 'The Viscountess's clothes are so smart that even well-dressed Melbourne is expected to rub its eyes when she emerges from Georgette's, and her enthusiasm should make her a success in her first venture into business.'

Before they embarked on their separate careers Jack and Cristina decided to go to Sydney for a few days' vacation and to meet an old friend of Jack's, Geoffrey Gibbs. The two men had been together at Eton and Oxford, and Gibbs had stayed for a time with Jack in Manchester Square before coming out to Brisbane to work in a branch of his family bank. The three of them spent most of their days on the beach, swimming at Bondi, Manly and Coogee, in the evenings the two men relaxing over a drink before dinner while Cristina played to them on her ukulele. This peaceful respite was enjoyable but brief. After less than a week they separated, Gibbs returning to Brisbane, Cristina to Melbourne, while Jack set off up country to begin his new life as a jackeroo.

The Yanko station in the Riverina, just over 200 miles due north of Melbourne, had been part of Sir Samuel Wilson's vast portfolio of properties in Queensland, Victoria and New South Wales. Although after his death sections of the Yanko had been sold, over 70,000 acres of it still remained, most of it owned by Maud through the terms of her marriage settlement. Her first furious reaction when she learned of Jack's elopement had been to cancel the arrangements for him to stay on the station, but she soon calmed down sufficiently to realise this would achieve very little. She was still extremely angry, but Jack was her son – '*badly* as you have hurt both of us Jack we must try to forgive you & help you' – and she now focused her considerable energies on salvaging the situation. Her lawyers in Melbourne, Blake & Riggall, were instructed to contact the overseer at the station and inform him that Lord Hastings '[had] the family consent to his going to the Yanko to gain experience, so long as it is perfectly clear that he interferes in no way with the management'. It was made equally clear that in no circumstances was Lady Hastings to set foot on any part of the property.

For Jack it was a long, hot journey by train, over 400 miles north-west from Sydney to the small town of Jerilderie in the south of the Riverina; here he was picked up in a truck for the final few miles along the rutted road to the station. The country was like nothing he had seen before, the vast skies, the dusty red plains patchily covered in scrubby grass, the occasional grove of parched gum trees, the outcrop of green along the banks of a creek. Arrival at the Yanko came as a pleasant surprise: through a gate, up a long sandy carriage-drive bordered by white picket-fencing and then suddenly there was the house, a large and handsome one-storey building encircled by a spacious veranda. Surrounded by a shady garden with green lawns, tall trees and well-tended flower beds, the house on one side looked over a fast-flowing creek, whose banks were overhung with willow and acacia. At the back of the house was an extensive yard with offices, stables, machinery and hay sheds, and a substantial storehouse which supplied half the region with dry foods, medicines and other necessities. Nearer to the house were the jackeroos' quarters, a pleasant dwelling also with a wide veranda, its entrance bordered by flowering shrubs. It was here that Jack spent his first night on the station.

My father sometimes talked of his time at the Yanko, and as a child I remember how impressed I was by his specialist skills. For many years my parents had a house in Hampshire, and it was here we sometimes saw the ex-jackeroo in action: he could lasso a pony, throw a boomerang, and when the neighbouring farmer's cows broke through into our garden, as they not infrequently did, my father with a strange yelping cry ('Heitch! Heitch!') would round them up with a whirl and crack of a stock-whip. Once, on a mountain path in North Wales when we came across a dying sheep, its belly an open wound seething with maggots, my father broke its neck with a powerful jerk of his wrist. He was given a hard time, he said, when he arrived at the Yanko, this seemingly effete young Englishman who'd never done a proper day's work in his life. On his first day on the station they gave him to ride a mean little brumby, only half broken, who bucked furiously the moment it was mounted. Luckily all those years in the saddle paid off: he rode out at a fast gallop and never had trouble with his work-mates again.

Already at the Yanko were three other jackeroos, all young public-school men come to gain experience before returning to work on their family stations. Well educated they may have been but they were worked very hard, their duties little different from those of the stockmen. Heading the hierarchy was the manager Mr Brownless, who had previously worked on another Wilson property. Mr Brownless, always immaculately turned out, was a kind man but he ran a tight ship and expected his employees to adhere to his own high standards. On most nights the jackeroos ate in their quarters, where they had their own cook to look after them, but once a week the four young men, in dark suits and ties, were invited to dine with Mr and Mrs Brownless where, seated round a mahogany dining-table, they were encouraged to make conversation on subjects other than drought, foot-rot and the rabbit problem.

Work was physically demanding and started immediately after an early breakfast. Jack, like the others, had five horses allotted him, whose care and condition were entirely his responsibility. After saddling up, the jackeroos in jodhpurs and wide-brimmed hats rode off down the drive, past the cook-house, past the vast, cathedral-like wool-shed, and out onto the wide open plains of the Riverina. They rode for hours over paddocks extending for thousands of acres, with the help of dogs and stock-whips mustering enormous mobs of prime Merino sheep. The animals were always in need of attention: there was the marking and docking of lambs, rescuing bogged ewes, and dealing with a wide variety of pests and diseases; there was also the endless inspection of miles of fencing erected in a vain attempt to keep out the millions of rabbits which were fast overrunning the country. By twilight it sometimes seemed as if the ground were moving, and Jack soon became used to the awful sight of 12-foot fences piled to the top with rabbit corpses, dead in their attempt to scramble over. Often the men covered as many as 40 miles a day, seeing nobody except occasionally on the great bullock wagons laden with bales of wool, or from time to time a solitary drover with his mongrel pack and little herd of cattle grazing meagrely on the side of the road.

Sometimes they rode too far to return by evening, remaining out for several days before coming back to the homestead. Then the men made camp by the side of a creek, boiling their billycans over the fire for tea, before grilling chops for supper with the inevitable accompaniment of dried peas and tinned fruit. In spite of the heat, the dust and the flies Jack came to love the endless skies, the arid plains that seemed to stretch for ever, the groves of red gum and cooba, the scent of wattle, and the exotic wildlife, kangaroo and koala, parrots and rose-breasted galahs, even occasional flocks of emu and ostrich. He used to describe lying on his swag, huddled up with blanket and mosquito net, looking up at the stars, with nothing to disturb the silence but the occasional stamp and snort of a tethered horse.

In contrast to this somewhat solitary existence was the shearing which began at the end of July and went on into August. During these intensely pressured weeks, the jackeroos were kept busy rounding up thousands of sheep and driving them into the pens at the foot of the massive, ochre wool-shed, where in the dark, strong-smelling interior the shearers were waiting for them. More usually, however, the working day ended at 5.00 p.m. when the men had just enough time to drive into Jerilderie and line up four

or five beers before the bars closed at 6.00 p.m. Then it was back
to the station for a hearty meal, and perhaps a game of cards and
listening to the gramophone before bed. Despite the remoteness,
there was a fair amount of recreation on Sundays, bush picnics,
tennis, cricket, even the occasional game of polo. There was also
plenty to read as the Brownlesses had a good library, and dozens
of newspapers and periodicals arrived with every post. For Jack
the weekly delivery of mail was not without its anxieties: it might
bring a diatribe from his mother, or a communication from her
lawyers in Melbourne; it would certainly bring a letter from
Cristina.

　　Two hundred miles away, Cristina was painfully missing her
husband. On one level she was kept fully occupied with a busy
social life and with her work at Georgette's: to be near the shop
she had taken a room in a gloomy red-brick building only a couple
of minutes' walk away on Flinders Lane, a narrow street in the
heart of the city. But she yearned for Jack, and the weeks between
his brief visits sometimes seemed endless. Meanwhile she, too,
was receiving admonishments from home. Her father, Camillo
Casati, for once stirred into involving himself in his daughter's
affairs, had sent her a letter of considered, even kindly advice;
any salutary effect was, however, undermined by his enclosing a
second letter, this one from a companion in arms of Maud's, which
was ferociously critical of Cristina's behaviour.

　　'Carissima Cristina,' Camillo began.

Siccome desidero talmente la tua felicità e voglio tu riprenda la
posizione che ti è dovuta in Inghilterra e che tu no continui ad essere
sempre una 'outsider', sento che è mio dovere inviarti la copia di una
lettera che ricevo da un amico nostro e che è pure amico delle famiglia
Huntington [sic]. Leggi bene la lettera, non con spirito di rivolta o di
'un enfichisme'. Una cosa certezza che questa lettera è stata scritta at
solo scopo del tuo bene ed è isperata da *puro affetto* per te.[16]

---

[16] 'Since I wish for your happiness above all and want you to resume the position that
is your due in England, I feel it is my duty to send you the copy of a letter I received

The letter reads suspiciously as if it had been dictated by Maud herself. Cristina should know that 'they are all watching her, & up to now the reports are *not* good … She must be *made to understand* that she must behave herself, & if she does, & if she makes the boy happy, her mother-in-law will be the first to turn & become her best friend … But if she goes on, as she does now, there is no hope for any reconciliation & they will be done for good.' After quoting the letter in full, Camillo ends by impressing on his daughter that the future is entirely in her hands. 'Con un po di coraggio e persistenza in Australia tuo marito puo riuscire magnificamente e la su Famiglia non solo ti amerà, ma ti ringraziera per il bene che avrai fatto a loro Figlio … Ricordami a tuo Marito e credere con grande affetto il tuo Papà.'[17]

How, and indeed if, Cristina replied to her father is not known, but her feelings are made clear by the comment scribbled in the margin: 'What fools!'

Living and working way up country, Jack was left alone by the press, but Cristina in Melbourne immediately became a focus of attention. That the wife of an English lord was working in a shop, albeit a notably stylish establishment, inevitably became a topic of fascinated speculation. 'The entry of the youthful Lady Hastings into the commercial life of Melbourne as saleswoman to a Collins Street modiste has caused more than a mild flutter in the fashionable homes of Toorak,'[18] began one of the many articles on the subject. 'The expected rush of high society shoppers will inevitably recall the battle of Hastings.' Cristina was repeatedly photographed and interviewed, dealing with the numerous intrusions in a coolly dignified manner. When asked why she had

---

from a friend of the Huntingdon family. Read the letter carefully, not in a spirit of revolt or of "couldn't care less" as this letter was definitely written entirely for your benefit and inspired by pure affection for you.'

[17] 'With a little courage and persistence in Australia your husband can succeed magnificently and his family will not only love you, but they will thank you for the good you will have done their son … Remember me to your husband and believe me with great affection, your Papa.'

[18] *The Register*, 6.2.26. Adelaide.

decided to go into the dress business, she replied, 'It is quite simple. There was time to fill in, and I have a flair for this sort of work … And no, I have not been trained. I suppose when one has always worn the right thing one gets – how shall I say? – a feeling.'[19] In private, however, she found the experience dispiriting; the publicity had brought in more customers, but disappointingly most came to gape rather than buy. 'I had a very busy day. I am dead beat & my feet are so sore,' she told Jack, 'but what stingy people, they just look at everything, try everything on & then get nothing. I made about 2 pounds percentage.'

Fortunately when away from Georgette's Cristina had the distraction of a busy social life. 'The fair, slim, beauteous wife of Lord Hastings'[20] was energetically pursued by local hostesses eager to make her acquaintance, and she was invited to luncheons and dinners, race meetings, picnics and garden parties, even to a ball at Government House. As when she was living in London, Cristina soon made a group of friends, party-loving young women and their husbands and escorts. Among them were Alvilde Bridges, whose father was Governor of South Australia; Joan Chirnside, the pretty daughter of a wealthy pastoralist, who, like Cristina, was an expert on the ukulele; Rosy Spowers, daughter of the newspaper proprietor William Spowers; and the politician Jack Duncan-Hughes and his wife: 'High class Australians the P&O kind that talk sloly not to go wrong in their accent!', as Cristina described them to Jack.

As a member of this lively band Cristina spent most of her spare time out on the town, often ending the evening dancing into the small hours in the city's nightclubs. 'I'm getting terribly social in your absence', she told her husband.

Yesterday we went up to Menzies to tea. All the jeunesse dorée was there some of the most presentable I've seen for some time … Tomorrow I lunch at Menzies with Rosy Spowers & Joan [Chirnside] & go to the

[19] *Sydney Morning Herald*, nd.
[20] Ibid.

Animal ball at the Embassy. I thought it ment that everybody would go dressed as animals, making animal noises, but no such luck its only for the benefit of the prevension of cruelty to animals.

This was all very well, and Cristina was glad not to spend much time alone in her lodgings, yet she painfully missed her husband. 'Oh pussy I want to be cuddled ever so tight & kissed ever so hard. You are much too far away, right up by a Bilabong under an unspreading eucaliptus tree ... please darling come back soon.' She constantly worried that Jack was working too hard and not taking care of himself, and she was full of curiosity about the station and about the people with whom Jack was living and working. 'Do please tell me all about Yanko what they are all like on ferther acquaintance ... Are sheep more interesting than they look?'

And yet although the refrain is one of pining and sadness at their separation – 'I'm very unhappy without you & don't seem to be getting used to it at all ... the more I go out & the more people I see, the more I want to be with you. I do feel so lonely without you' – and although Jack's letters, as always, were 'triumphs of uncommunicativeness', none the less relations between husband and wife at this period appear to have been both loving and serene. In spite of their separation, Cristina appears confident of her husband's feelings for her, teasing him affectionately and doing her best to entertain him and make him laugh. She frequently decorated her letters with saucy drawings and copied out a number of risqué rhymes to amuse him.

> There were three young ladies of Birmingham
> And this is the story concerning them
> Those naughty young flirts
> Took down ther skirts
> In front of the Bishop conferming them.
> But the Bishop was no bloody fool
> He had been to a good public school
> So he downed with his breeches

And rushed at those bitches
With yards of episcopal spool!

Because the distances were so great and Jack's time off was limited,
the couple met only infrequently; Cristina of course was forbidden
to visit the Yanko but Jack came to Melbourne whenever he had
a few days' freedom. While together, Cristina delighted in introducing him to her friends and he revelled in the comforts and
amenities of city life, in such marked contrast to the small world of
the sheep station. For Jack it was a welcome change to dine in good
restaurants, to have a drink at the august Melbourne Club, where
his grandfather, Sir Sam, had been such a prominent member, to
see a play and go to the movies. In particular he enjoyed visiting
the city's art galleries.

Uppermost in Jack's mind was still his ambition to paint, an
ambition unlikely to be realised while he continued to work as a
jackeroo. But neither he nor Cristina had intended to remain in
Australia for ever: recently they had begun to talk of visiting one
of the islands of the French Pacific, not only to see for themselves
their legendary beauty but also as a form of homage to Paul
Gauguin, whose ruthless rejection of his bourgeois existence had
made him a hero to Jack. His sister Marian and her husband had
recently spent a few weeks on Tahiti while on their way back from
Europe to the Falklands, and Marian had written enthusiastically
of the island's beauty and leisurely way of life. Her account had
made a deep impression on Jack, who had long fantasised about
living on a tropical island: as a boy he had been entranced by the
stories of Herman Melville and Robert Louis Stevenson, before
more recently falling under the spell of Gauguin, whose work he
had first seen at the Tate Gallery in London. As for Gauguin, so for
Jack the prospect of abandoning the restrictions of a conventional
way of life for the freedom of the tropics seemed irresistible.

It was while Jack was in Melbourne that what had up to now
seemed no more than a dream suddenly began to materialise.
One evening while with a group of friends at the Victorian Artists'

Society in Albert Street he was introduced to the celebrated painter, William Blamire Young. Then in his late fifties, Blamire Young was an English-Australian artist who in the 1890s had studied painting in London with, among others, James Pryde and William Nicholson. After many years of struggle and poverty, Young finally won recognition in his adopted country as one of the most important painters of his era – his works hung in several State galleries and he was commissioned to design the first stamps for the Commonwealth of Australia; admired for his painting, he was also greatly respected as the art critic of the Melbourne *Herald*, much in demand for lectures and after-dinner speeches.

Tall, good-looking, voluble and charming, the older man was an engaging companion, sympathetic to Jack's artistic aspirations. The two quickly developed a friendship, with Blamire Young encouraging Jack to believe he could earn his living as a painter; he advised him, however, to leave the southern hemisphere and take some course of study either in Europe or the United States.

By a stroke of great good fortune it was exactly at this point that Jack learned he was the recipient of a generous bequest: his grand-mother, old Lady Wilson, who had died a few months earlier, had left him £3,000 (now worth nearly £400,000), a sum that suddenly made possible this new adventure.

With Cristina's enthusiastic support, Jack began planning their future. Neither was ready to return home, both were eager to visit America, Jack in particular keen to see something of the lively art scene in southern California. The mail ships en route from Sydney to San Francisco stopped at Tahiti, and thus nothing would be easier than to spend two or three months there before continuing to the States. After much discussion between them, Jack returned to the Yanko, where he was soon followed by a letter from Cristina, charmingly decorated with a drawing of herself lying naked under a coconut palm. 'I do hope we will be able to go away soon', she wrote yearningly. 'Oh darling those south sea islands seem more & more attractive, the more one thinks about them. I'm simply longing to lye in the sun with no work to be done.'

When preparing to leave the Yanko, Jack was naturally under obligation to communicate with his mother's lawyers in Melbourne; true to form, the information was kept to the minimum, Blake & Riggall told only that Lord Hastings would shortly be leaving Australia and would be spending an unspecified time in the South Pacific.

When the news was communicated to Maud she was appalled. This disastrous scheme was all Cristina's doing, of course: '[Cristina] now wants to go off to the South Sea Islands, & make him give up his work', she complained angrily to a friend. 'That will *absolutely finish him*. He is safe where he is now ... well looked after by well-to-do people, & if he persisted bravely he may become a very rich man. The boy is clever, but weak. The climate of the South Sea Islands will simply ruin him & he will become a beachcomber.'

Meanwhile Jack and Cristina continued to make preparations for departure. Finally visas were arranged, possessions packed, leave taken of all their friends, and on 7 September 1926 the Hastingses in Sydney boarded the mail-ship that called in every month en route to San Francisco. Two weeks later they disembarked at Papeete on the island of Tahiti. 'I was travelling from Australia to the US and "stopped off"', Jack wrote afterwards. 'I liked it so much that I "stopped off" for some considerable time.'

5

'An episode out of another life'

The RMS *Makura* docked at Papeete early in the morning. The ship was slowly winched in alongside the little quay already packed with a colourful crowd of locals, a throng of sun helmets, white duck, straw hats and brightly patterned dresses excitedly waiting for the arrival of friends and the delivery of mail. The bustle and noise, the hooting of cars and ringing of bicycle bells, the sweet stench of drying copra, the heat already beating down on the corrugated iron roofs of the warehouses provided a marked contrast to the island's appearance just after dawn. From the ship's deck Jack and Cristina had had their first sight of the incomparable beauty of Tahiti: beyond the white line of the reef the island rose out of a dark blue sea, its mountain peaks embedded in forest and wreathed in cloud, with just visible in the distance the dramatic spires and pinnacles of the neighbouring island of Moorea.

As soon as the smartly uniformed French officials had made their inspection, the passengers – the usual diverse group, as Jack referred to them, 'of sightseers, drunks, pearl merchants, old maiden ladies, traders, seasoned travellers, writers and artists'[21] – were free to disembark. The new arrivals soon dispersed, heading off to explore 'the tiny pagan city', as Robert Louis Stevenson had described it in the 1890s. Now, however, although little expanded in size, Papeete could hardly be described as pagan,

---

[21] Unpublished ms, HRC.

with numbers of churches of various denominations and even a miniature cathedral. Immediately back from the waterfront was the tree-shaded main street of small shops mostly run by Chinese, and behind these the centre of town, with cafés, several restaurants and hotels, offices, and the Cercle Bougainville, the eminently respectable members-only club for the local schooner captains, pearl buyers and traders. Further out were the consulates, dignified residences set in luxuriant gardens and surrounded by leafy neighbourhoods of small houses, their verandas heavily draped in purple bougainvillea.

On the outskirts of town were the poorer, native communities, with extended families living in small huts surrounded by cats, dogs, pigs, poultry, cows and horses. Thick foliage grew everywhere, acacia, jacaranda and scarlet-blossomed flamboyant trees, dense shrubberies of oleander, hibiscus and the waxen white Tiare Tahiti, the flower ineradicably associated with the islands and with the paintings of Gauguin.

With no particular plan in mind the Hastingses decided to spend a few days in Papeete and then perhaps hire a car and explore the rest of the island. But one evening while sitting on the veranda of the Mariposa Café they fell into conversation with a Danish sea captain. He owned a small yacht, he told them, and offered to take them on a voyage round some of the nearer atolls and islands before they made up their minds where they wanted to settle. Delighted, they agreed, and set off the next day from the very quay at which they had so recently arrived.

But after only a couple of hours a sudden storm blew up, forcing the skipper to take shelter on the nearest island, Moorea. Once landed, Jack and Cristina were instantly bewitched by the almost unbelievable beauty of the landscape before them, a beauty so perfect it appeared like a dream, a fantasy of a Pacific island: here were white coral beaches fringed with coconut palms, behind which forests of mango trees rose up from grassy slopes which in turn, in Jack's words, 'led to the towering crags of blue-grey volcanic rock which stretch up as needles and knife edges, thousands of feet above the sea'.[22] Both decided that this was where they wanted to live.

Returned to Papeete they consulted an estate agent who by great good fortune had a house for sale on his books. Faretaotootoa belonged to a retired English naval officer, J. R. Grey, who with his Australian wife had bought the 40-acre property seven years earlier. The Greys had developed the previously neglected coconut and vanilla plantations, and had built a house out of coral right on the waterfront, a spacious single-storey building shaded by palm trees. A wide veranda and a steeply overhanging roof kept the interior cool; indoors were 12 rooms, including an airy sitting-room, a library with a fireplace, and a modern bathroom with a water-heater, a luxury then almost unknown in the tropics. There was a well-tended garden, with hibiscus and oleander as well as guava, mangoes, banana and a pineapple patch, and this led down to the beach and a little jetty where a sailing canoe was kept; moored in the bay was a small yacht, *White Heather*. To run the household were three servants, a houseboy and cook, both Chinese, and a Tahitian maid, Nadia. The Hastingses were entranced and bought the property on sight. Soon afterwards Cristina had a visiting card printed which read simply, 'Viscountess Hastings—Moorea—Pacific Ocean'.

Looking back at his life in the South Seas, Jack always described it as an earthly paradise; it was, he said, 'an episode out of another life', an idyllic period completely different from anything he had known before or would experience again. In the words of one of the novelists of the period, Moorea 'had the air of a world withdrawn',[23] and the Hastingses responded gratefully not only to the perfect climate but to the slow pace and quiet of the island, the lack of crowds and noise.

Both were spellbound by the beauty surrounding them, by the blue, green and purple of the lagoon, with its brilliantly coloured

---

[22] Ibid.
[23] *Numerous Treasure*, Robert Keable (Hurst & Blackett, 1925) p. 15.

fish forever darting in and out of the coral; with the white beaches and swaying coconut palms, with behind them lush groves of mango and avocado, interspersed with brilliant bursts of hibiscus, oleander and white tiare. In the interior were ferns and dense forest and clear-running streams, and the formidable fastness of the jagged mountain peaks rising dramatically from the centre. Sitting on the veranda in the evening they could look far out to sea, the Southern Cross low in the sky, and listen to the rustle of palm fronds and the distant thunder of waves breaking on the reef.

Time passed seamlessly. In the mornings after an early swim Jack often took his canoe and joined the local men fishing in the lagoon, or went with them into the interior hunting wild boar, or at night wading up the sandy rivers by torchlight spearing eel and shrimp. Sometimes he and Cristina spent the day sailing in their little yacht round the island, or out into the open waters of the Pacific. It was not all recreation, however, and there was always plenty of work to be done: for Jack overseeing the plantation and organising the transport and marketing of copra and vanilla, and for Cristina the entirely novel experience of housekeeping. At such a distance from the mainland a careful eye had to be kept on provisions: a schooner made the three-hour journey from Papeete twice a week bringing supplies and it was essential to know well in advance how much meat, butter and ice to order. 'Such a mundane word as house-keeping probably never enters one's mind in connection with the South Seas,' she remarked in a newspaper interview, 'yet keep house I did.'

For both husband and wife, this period together on Moorea was certainly the most tranquil of their marriage. There were fewer than a dozen expatriates living on the island, and for the first time Cristina had Jack almost entirely to herself. They both loved the place, were free to do whatever they wanted, free of the pressures and strains of their previous existence. For Jack it was a relief to see Cristina happy, and in her present contented state he was able to enjoy her company without the constant dread of her temper. Now at last he was able to devote much of his time to painting: he spent hours with his easel on the beach or wandering into the interior with his sketchbook from which he would then work when back at the house. They both swam several times a day, Cristina gardened with enthusiasm, they read for hours, and Cristina played her ukulele while Jack took up the guitar.

There are photographs of this period showing him dressed in a pareo sitting on the veranda smiling with his guitar on his knee; others are of Cristina in the garden, slender and elegant in a sleeveless linen shift and coolie hat, feeding her doves; they are together at a native feast with wreaths round their heads; sailing on *White Heather*; sitting in the canoe, their feet dangling in the water; relaxing comfortably indoors in an airy white room whose walls are hung with a collection of boomerangs, a couple of crocodile skins and a big patterned Tahitian bark-cloth. The only other expatriate couple on the island were Medford and Gladys Kellum, both American, who had arrived a couple of years previously; the Hastingses and Kellums saw each other regularly, Cristina and Gladys particularly glad of each other's company in such a predominantly male environment.

Once a month, when the two mail-ships came in from Sydney and San Francisco, the Hastingses in their little yacht made the often very choppy 15-mile crossing to Papeete. Here they collected letters from home, books, magazines and gramophone records; they visited the market, the tailor's, went to the movies, and met friends for a drink or dinner in one of the many bars and restaurants. The town was always crowded on these occasions, a mix of Europeans and Chinese with the dark-skinned Tahitians, the men in shirts and cotton trousers, the women with their long dark hair loose down their backs, in straw hats and colourful if shapeless cotton dresses.

Tahiti during the 1920s had become something of a magnet, particularly for artists and writers, drawn by the likes of Stevenson, Gauguin and Rupert Brooke. The island's expatriate community was intensely social, and in a very short time Jack and Cristina had made a number of friends, among them the well-known novelist,

Zane Grey, the painters George Biddle, Francis McComas and Paul Engdahl, and two Americans, Charles Nordhoff and James Norman Hall, who were shortly to win international fame with their novel, *Mutiny on the Bounty*.

For Jack one of the most interesting among the island community was the English writer and artist, Robert Keable. Keable, just 40, was an ex-Church of England vicar who had left both his wife and his ministry, and was now settled on Tahiti with a Tahitian mistress. Keable's first work of fiction, *Simon Called Peter*, had been a runaway success, but the book of his Jack most admired, which indeed made a lasting impression, was *Numerous Treasure*, published in 1925, a richly sensuous story of a callow young Englishman arrived on a South Sea island who falls in love with a beautiful native girl. A sub-plot in the book, also much applauded by Jack, was Keable's attack on the Christian missionaries, who forced the Tahitian women to abandon their traditional semi-nakedness for the cumbersome 'mother hubbards' which covered them almost from neck to ankle.

In April 1927, six months after the Hastingses had left Australia, the painter, Blamire Young, Jack's old mentor from Melbourne, arrived on Moorea. The two had been corresponding about a joint project, a collection of Polynesian stories to be written by Jack and illustrated by Blamire Young. 'Though our efforts may not possess the exotic allure of Paul Gauguin yet something may appear that will at any rate give some pleasure to ourselves,'[24] Young had told him. The few weeks Young spent at Faretaotootoa were both productive and enjoyable, the two men painting and talking about painting, with Jack also working on the stories and planning their shared oeuvre – 'a very happy collaboration,'[25] as Young described it.

After Blamire Young left, Jack gave his script to Robert Keable for comment. Unfortunately Keable's response, if courteous, was far from encouraging.

---

[24] Blamire Young to JH 22.2.27. HRC.
[25] Blamire Young to JH 18.1.28. HRC.

My dear Hastings … Are these stories really so beautiful or interesting? … From the point of view of artistic perception and beauty,
most of them fail in your telling … Frankly, I think by far your best
chance is to try to get them into the Xmas TATLER or SKETCH …
Lastly, if you will forgive me, I should type them double spaced and
just look again at the punctuation and some of the spellings.[26]

If not overly impressed, Keable was none the less supportive,
even sending the manuscript to his own publisher in London, the
scholarly Michael Sadleir at Constable. Sadleir turned it down,
but *The Golden Octopus: Legends of the South Seas* was published
the following year, 1928, by Nash & Grayson, in a remarkably
handsome edition which unfortunately attracted little attention.
'Viscount Hastings, the most interesting recent recruit to the
lotus-eating European community of the South Seas, has registered his reactions to this idyllic environment in a truly delectable
form', began one of the few brief reviews to appear. 'Gauguin's
name is misspelt in the preface, but we have noticed no other
typographical blunder.' Despite Blamire Young's reputation, the
book did little better in Australia, although Young, who remained
proud of the work, was pleased to report that in Melbourne one
of the first to buy a copy was Cristina's old employer, the owner of
Georgette's.

Three months before Blamire Young's stay on Moorea, a young
Englishman had arrived in Papeete on his second visit to the
island. Alec Waugh, then aged 29, was a writer, elder brother
of the soon-to-be-famous Evelyn, whom Jack had known very
slightly at Oxford – and whom he was shortly to provide with
some family detail for his new novel, *Vile Bodies*.[27] Alec, who
largely subsidised his career as a novelist by contributing travel
articles to American magazines, had visited Tahiti for the first

---

[26] Robert Keable to JH 21.6.27. HRC.
[27] At the end of the novel, Colonel Blount, the heroine's father, makes a film about the
eighteenth-century Methodist, Selina, Countess of Huntingdon, and the two rivals for
her love, Wesley and Whitefield. At the end of the film, Wesley in America 'is rescued
from Red Indians by Lady Huntingdon disguised as a cowboy'.

time the previous year when he had met and fallen in love with an attractive American woman, Ruth Morris, wife of Gouverneur Morris, a well-to-do screenwriter based in California. Now Ruth and 'Govie' were due to return to the island, and Alec, by a combination of luck and careful planning, had arranged to reach Papeete shortly before them.

It was at this point, in January 1927, that Jack and Alec first met, a meeting that marked the beginning of a lifetime's devoted friendship. Alec, small, dapper, quietly spoken, always smelling slightly of an expensive Russian Leather soap, was an engaging figure; insatiably curious, intelligent, amusing, he was also, like Jack, an intensely private person beneath the courteous manner. The Hastingses invited him to stay at Faretaotootoa, the visit a great success with all three. Alec was fascinated by the relationship between husband and wife, alert to the potentially dangerous differences between them. 'Cristina', he recalled, 'was a wild creature of the jungle with dark skin and prominent white teeth. Her excitement was infectious. Hastings was the complete opposite. He was tall, apparently mild in manner but forceful in argument. They were excellent foils to one another.'[28]

When the Morrises eventually arrived, Alec introduced them, and the two couples quickly became friends. Govie, dark-haired and bespectacled, a cigarette always on the go, was a genial character, a respected writer of short stories as well as of scripts for the movies, a substantial figure both intellectually and in physique; in his fifties he was over 20 years older than his attractive second wife. Ruth, small and slender, already had an impressive career behind her: she, too, worked as a script-writer, could fly a plane – during the war she had held a commission in the army to train pilots – drove a racing car and had trained as a matador in Madrid. Wild and wilful by nature, she had had a number of lovers, among whom the deeply enamoured Alec was the latest.

---

[28] *The Best Wine Last*, Alec Waugh (W. H. Allen, 1978) p. 55.

While conducting his secret love affair with Ruth, Alec remained on Tahiti for nearly nine months, during which time he stayed on at least one occasion with the Hastingses on Moorea. He had arranged to sail for California in October, and was surprised and delighted to learn that Jack and Cristina would be on the same ship. They had decided to return for a while to England, the purpose of the trip, it appeared, so that Jack could oversee publication of *The Golden Octopus*: the real reason, however, was that Cristina was three months' pregnant.

After disembarking in San Francisco, the Hastingses spent a couple of days at the luxurious St Francis Hotel with Alec, before going on to Pebble Beach for a brief stay with two fellow passengers, the painter Francis McComas and his wife, who, like the Morrises, were regular visitors to Tahiti. At the beginning of November they left California, travelling by train to New York to meet the ship that was to take them across the Atlantic.

Arrived at Southampton, they were met by the usual group of journalists eager for society gossip. 'Viscount and Viscountess Hastings, who have spent two years honeymooning in a delightful coral house in the South Sea Islands, were radiantly happy when they arrived at Southampton recently', began one report. 'Their happiness was the greater because of the reconciliation that has taken place between Lord Hastings and his family.' When pressed on the subject, the Viscount stated, 'My family are now quite reconciled, and we are looking forward to a very cordial reception at home.'

The terms 'radiantly happy' and 'quite reconciled' were perhaps not strictly accurate. Certainly it was true that since Jack's hurried departure two years earlier the Huntingdons' attitude towards him had softened, largely due to the efforts of his two older sisters. Both Kathleen and Norah had worked tirelessly to persuade their parents, in particular their mother, to forgive their errant son. This Maud was now prepared to do, and it was generally accepted that at least a façade of good relations should be maintained. Jack and Cristina were invited to stay at Burton, and dutifully they went, but their visits were not a success. Maud took little trouble to conceal the fact that she loathed her daughter-in-law and held her almost entirely to blame for Jack's failure to make a successful career, while Cristina, completely unafraid, made no secret of her contempt for Maud.

It wasn't long before Maud was telling her exactly what she thought. 'Dear Cristina', begins one highly charged missive.

> I never *shirk* my duty & I *consider* it my duty to try & make you *realize* the situation … I know you will weep & have hysterics quite easily, but it means *nothing* to you … There are *tragedies* in life much too deep for casual tears, but they break the *heart*. Jack is our *only* son, the last representative of a great name … He was such a good straight sound fellow with high ideals & principles … Alas all seems changed since his marriage … No chance any more of honourable directorships or other positions of trust but drab surroundings in some drear lodging among sleazy companions with all inspiration gone … It is all *too too* sad.

The 'drear lodging' referred to was in fact an elegant furnished apartment which had been lent them in Cumberland Terrace, one of the beautiful Nash terraces built around the Outer Circle in Regent's Park. The interior Cristina had arranged with her instinctive flair while Jack had hung a couple of his Tahitian paintings over the mantelpieces in the sitting- and dining-room. At the beginning of January 1928, following the advice of Blamire Young, Jack began a course at the Slade School of Fine Art, then under the leadership of the formidable Henry Tonks. Before Jack was accepted, Tonks had interviewed him and looked favourably on the selection of drawings and water-colours presented for his inspection.

To Jack's surprise Tonks, famous for his caustic remarks, had proved both friendly and encouraging. He talked about the importance of drawing and recommended that Jack study the Italian painters of the sixteenth century, '[as they] will always be the best school for those who want to learn what drawing

Maud Huntingdon resplendent as the Spirit of Australia

Warner Huntingdon, Master of Foxhounds

Jack in costume as the ideal son and heir

Maud decoratively surrounded by her three daughters

Jack on leaving school

Jack taking a break at a point-to-point

Cristina in the South Seas

Jack and Cristina at Faretaotootoa

Caroline Condon in the south of France

Diego Rivera at work in the San Francisco Stock Exchange

Jack, Clifford Wight, Rivera and Dr Valentiner in Detroit
(courtesy of the Detroit Institute of Arts)

Frida Kahlo with Jean Abbott and Cristina

Jack in his St John's Wood studio, his portrait of Luisa Casati on the easel

Moorea meeting the Atherstone pack

Maud at Burton presiding at a garden fête

Jack and Margaret with their two daughters, Caroline and Selina

can explain.'[29] Although Jack completed only a couple of terms, he found his time at the Slade a rewarding experience, and was delighted to be told later by Tonks that from the first he had detected in his pupil a 'definite gift'.[30]

On 4 March 1928 Cristina gave birth to a daughter, who was named, after the place of her conception, Moorea. Neither parent showed much interest in her, Cristina, like her mother, wholly lacking in maternal instinct, while Jack, in common with many men of his class and generation, regarded babies almost as another species. The fact that both of them as children had had few demonstrations of affection, or indeed much personal contact of any kind, with their own parents must have added to their sense of detachment. A nurse was engaged to look after the child, and otherwise days at Cumberland Terrace passed very much as before, Jack attending his classes while Cristina devoted herself to a glamorous social life. 'Society is very interested just now in the novel parties which Lady Hastings is giving to the circle of friends she has gathered round her so quickly', one columnist reported, and 'Lady Hastings of the Titian hair' was soon to be seen at most of the smartest events of the season. Sometimes she was accompanied by her husband, but increasingly the Hastingses were leading separate lives, Jack largely uninterested in Cristina's social ambitions, while at home he was ever more alienated by her explosive temper and by what she herself, in a moment of contrition, referred to as her 'harpy naggin'.

Harpy naggers are rarely happy, and Cristina must have been made wretched by the increasing gap which she saw opening up between herself and her husband. For Jack, the truth was unavoidable: his runaway marriage had been a mistake; and while for a brief period on their tropical island he and Cristina had managed to live in comparative harmony, since their return

---

[29] *The Life of Henry Tonks*, Joseph Hone (Heinemann, 1939) p. 172.
[30] Henry Tonks to JH 7.9.34. HRC.

home he understood all too clearly that in temperament they were hopelessly incompatible. Equally clearly, he saw little prospect of escape: Cristina was emotionally dependent on him and intensely possessive; without her consent, divorce was impossible; and with the birth of their child they were further bound together. It was at this point that Jack met the woman who was to become one of the two great loves of his life.

Caroline Condon was an American divorcée, rich, intelligent and very beautiful. By her ex-husband, Edward B. Condon, she had two small sons with whom she moved between London (Belgrave Square), Paris (rue de Varenne) and a villa in the south of France. Caroline was sociable, chic and extremely *sportive*: she skated, she skied and, an expert horsewoman, hunted regularly in both England and France. It was in London that she and Jack met, introduced by an old friend of Jack's from Oxford, Alfred Beit, who in the past had pursued Caroline, although without much success. Jack was very much taken not only by the ravishing appearance of this slender, dark-haired young woman, but by her fearlessness, intelligence and good nature.

The affair began almost at once, and in conditions of the utmost secrecy. Jack's side of the correspondence has of course disappeared, but many of Caroline's letters remain, discreetly addressed to him at the Bachelors' Club, off Piccadilly, of which he had been a member since leaving university. The sequence of events is difficult to track as most of the correspondence is undated, but there is no doubt the relationship was both passionate and profound; Jack for the first time fell deeply in love, and had circumstances been different it is entirely possible that he and Caroline might have married.

During the autumn of 1928, the two of them met secretly and whenever they could, either in London or at house parties in the country or, very occasionally, at Caroline's apartment in Paris. Inevitably their assignations are followed by poignant expressions of missing and longing and eager anticipation of the next rendezvous. 'My darling, It seems incredible that you were actually here two days ago I have felt *so* miserable since you left!' Caroline wrote to him from the rue de Varenne. 'You looked so funny & sweet in your blue pyjamas … Jack darling write me please everything!! I miss you so! Those two days were heavenly but too short! I long so for you.'

At the beginning it appears that Jack, expert since childhood at emotional concealment, was able to keep from Cristina any hint of what was going on. But then in January 1929 he and Caroline devised a plan by which the Hastingses should come out to Switzerland to ski and as it were by chance stay at the same hotel as Caroline, who would be in a small party of friends, including Alfred Beit, self-appointed chaperon and confidant.

Inevitably the arrangement ended in disaster. Caroline and Alfred had been installed at the Palace Hotel in St Moritz for several days when the Hastingses arrived. At first all went well: there are photographs of the four of them skiing, sitting together in a horse-drawn sled, even one of Caroline and Cristina smiling while walking side by side through the snow. But at some point Cristina's suspicions were aroused; enraged, she confronted her husband; there was a furious row resulting in Jack's departure the following morning, alone, for London.

They were all very shaken, as Caroline's letters make clear.

Such a nightmare as the last few days have been! I cannot imagine anything more horrible. How did you get back to England? I hope you were not too miserable & upset & that now you are not unhappy. I think I should have willingly given every possession on earth to have made it less difficult & unpleasant for you that awful day you left … The one thought that obsesses me is that you are gone. Everything is *so* empty. I love you beyond everything on earth.

Shortly after Jack's departure Cristina, 'demented with intention to kill', stormed into Caroline's room, screaming at her that she was an 'American whore' who had been relentlessly pursuing her husband. Caroline, backed up by Alfred, who was also present, steadfastly denied the accusation. 'She has *no* proof of anything,'

Caroline reassured Jack, '& please excepting what you have already said *admit nothing more* … Everything will be used against us.'

The situation had indeed become dangerous. In those days when for a woman divorce was considered scandalous and a rumour of adultery could result in social exile and permanent disgrace, discretion and concealment were essential. Caroline, who had not only her reputation but also her children to consider, was extremely anxious that nothing should get out about her vituperative exchange with Cristina, which only Alfred had seen.

For this reason, she told Jack, it was vital to keep Alfred 'on side'.

> Remember he was the only eye witness … & when a Lady Cunard or a Lady Ribblesdale turns to Alfred & says we hear this & that etc etc, tell us what really happened, it is not such a bad thing to have Alfred on one's side. Cristina would say I was too careful of my reputation; perhaps you think so too. Nevertheless I should still like to keep a few friends in London whenever I care to go there again.

But Jack, it seems, had little need for advice on how to handle the crisis. During the impassioned confrontation with Cristina he had admitted his affair with Caroline, and partly in reparation had promised not to see her again for at least the next six months. This, he acknowledged, would be extremely difficult for them both, but he knew very well he was in the wrong and also understood all too clearly what Cristina was going through: his wife was in the painful position of being in love with a man who no longer loved her. When he broached the subject of a temporary separation to Caroline, she responded with character- istic generosity.

> Darling darling Do you know me so little that you think I hold you responsible for all the unpleasantness this affair has caused … It is such a good idea to promise C.H. not to see me for six months. You must do it at once it will set her mind at peace & will probably make life more possible for you dearest Jack … Don't think of me. Anything you did I would understand & I could never help loving you.

It was probably shortly after this that for the first time Jack talked to Cristina seriously about the possibility, if not of ending the marriage then at least of living apart. She, however, refused to discuss it, and so for the moment an uneasy peace was declared, with the Hastingses on one level continuing their shared existence while under the surface the tensions continued to fester.

Although he rarely spoke of her, it was a long time before Jack properly recovered from his love affair with Caroline. For the rest of his life he kept with him a tiny gold charm she had given him, and it was in commemoration of Caroline that nearly two decades later he gave her name to his youngest daughter. Caroline herself eventually remarried, to an American ranch-owner in Arizona, and it was nearly 30 years after the dénouement in St Moritz that Jack wrote to her there, sending her the letters of Abelard and Heloise, whose tragic love story had scandalised twelfth-century Paris. 'It was really sweet of you to have thought of me after so many years', Caroline replied. 'I often think of our happy days at St Moritz. (Not quite so happy in spots.) ... Unhappily I broke my neck and I am semi-paralysed – riding, of course ... I heard some time ago that you are happily married to a very nice woman.'

The term at the Slade finished at the end of May 1929, and Jack immediately began making plans to return to the South Pacific. It had never been his intention to stay away for long, and now that his affair with Caroline had in effect come to an end, he was impatient to be gone. Recently he and Cristina had received a letter from a young Tahitian woman they had befriended, her words a plangent reminder of what they had left behind. 'J'espère que vous reviendrez encore á Moorea dans votre petite maison qui vous attend avec patience', Téura Terii had written. 'Tellement je pense á vous et des fois les larmes me viennent aux yeux en voyant la maison Faretaotootoa, et personne dedans.'[31] As marital relations were so strained it was agreed between them that they

---

[31] 'I hope you will return to your little house on Moorea that so patiently awaits you. I think of you so often and at times tears come to my eyes when I see Faretaotootoa house and no-one inside.'

should have a breathing space, that Jack should leave on his own at the end of September, while Cristina would cross the Atlantic a few weeks later to join him in New York.

Meanwhile, arrangements had to be made for the care of their daughter as neither parent believed their peripatetic way of life was suitable for an 18-month-old child. Taking a deep breath, Jack went down to Burton to talk to his mother, first to break it to her that he would again be leaving the country, and second to ask her to look after Moorea.

Maud was deeply shocked by the news. She was appalled that her son, whom she had believed was at last beginning to settle down, was off again on his travels. It was all Cristina's fault, of course, as she had no hesitation in telling her; she was, however, far from dismayed by the prospect of taking charge of her grand-daughter. By her own lights, she had been an exemplary mother to her four children, and she was delighted she now had the chance to rescue Moorea from a deplorably bohemian environment and bring her up in a style suitable to her social standing.

For Jack, a friendship that had become important to him was that first formed on Tahiti with Alec Waugh. Alec had returned to London and he and the Hastingses had been frequently in each other's company. 'I suppose that ninety per cent of the really happy times I've had in the last two years have been bound up in some way or another with you both', Alec wrote fondly to them. He and Jack had discussed a plan of returning to Tahiti together, but at the time of Jack's planned departure Alec had family problems to cope with – his brother Evelyn's marriage was fast disintegrating and soon to end in divorce – which he felt prevented him from leaving the country.

However, as an experienced traveller, Alec was more than ready to give advice: instead of going straight to the States, he suggested, Jack should take a passage on one of the banana boats en route to Jamaica, and spend two or three weeks in the Caribbean before heading to New York. Furnished with Alec's letters of introduction, Jack arrived in Kingston on the SS *Jamaica Producer* at the beginning of September. He spent his first few days with Sir James Swettenham, a former Governor, then took off by himself to sketch in the north of the island, returning for his final week to stay with an American family living on Montego Bay.

The daughter of the house, Betty Sturges, tall and slim, with a mane of tawny blonde hair, was vivacious, fun and very, very pretty. Cheerful and kind-hearted, Betty loved men, she loved parties and firmly believed she'd been put on earth to have a good time, a belief which never wavered throughout her subsequent five marriages. She and Jack hit it off at once, almost immediately embarking on an affair which, light-hearted and enjoyable, was to turn into a friendship that lasted a lifetime. Jack was charmed and amused by Betty's wiles, and certainly found her attractive, while she was immensely taken by this cute young English lord with his immaculate manners, old-world accent and romantic stories of the South Seas. After Jack left, Betty wrote to him, 'Jack dear, I miss you frightfully & do hope you'll come back this way. Wish I wasn't quite so crazy about you and that circumstances were different. *Don't* fall in love & forget all about me & *do* write me sometime.' Although both assumed it would be, at best, a long while before they met again, in fact their next encounter, in rather different circumstances, was to be in the surprisingly near future.

At the end of September Jack arrived in New York to meet Cristina off her ship. Together they travelled by train to San Francisco, where, after a couple of nights at the St Francis Hotel, they boarded RMS *Tahiti* for the week's voyage back to the islands.

6

A fine prospect of the New World

Only very occasionally did my father talk about his life in the South Seas, and when he did, he seemed slightly surprised that we should be interested. As my mother once wrote, '[Jack] never dwells on personal reminiscence, and has an economical, half diffident way of bringing out, when pressed, the most surprising and recondite information.'[32] If verbal testimony were sparse, however, there were a few mementos, some physical evidence of his past life on Moorea, which he kept as souvenirs in his studio: two cowrie shells and a shimmering piece of mother-of-pearl on the window-sill; a little Polynesian figure, five inches tall, standing upright on a bookshelf; and over the fireplace a reproduction of *Arearea*, Gauguin's mysterious, semi-mythical portrait of two Tahitian women.

Most entrancing for my sister and myself were the occasions when he would take up his guitar and sing the first song he had learned while on the island, 'Three Blind Mice', in Hawaiian, for some reason:

> Ekolu 'iole makapo
> Ekolu 'iole makapo
> Ike I ka holo o lakou
> Ike I ka holo o lakou ...

Yet it wasn't until we were older, just into our teens, that the most exciting story came to light, a story that was eventually to involve

---

[32] *A Calabash of Diamonds*, Margaret Lane (Heinemann, 1961) p. 13.

both my parents in a highly dangerous and arguably nefarious expedition: a search for buried treasure in Mozambique.

The agent through whom my father had bought his house was an Englishman, Samuel Russell. Russell's office was in Papeete but he himself lived on Moorea with a Tahitian wife, and although he was much older, then in his late sixties, he and my father became friends. In the early years of the century, Russell had been a prospector, searching for gold and other minerals in Africa, and during his travels he had come across the story of a calabash of buried diamonds. While planning to investigate, the war intervened, and afterwards he had fallen ill and was now too old and frail to contemplate such an expedition. With no son of his own, Russell passed the story on to Jack, drawing a rough map of where the treasure, buried with the bones of a Zulu chieftain, was believed to lie, and urging him one day to go in search of it.

My father put the map away in a box of papers which eventually returned with him to England; here it lay undisturbed for 30 years in a vault in Barclays Bank until he happened to mention it one day as a curious footnote to one of his South Sea tales. My mother, always alert for adventure, was instantly intrigued, and in 1958 persuaded her husband to mount an expedition to Mozambique, an adventure which entailed considerable subterfuge, extreme danger and which very nearly ended in disaster.

Her account of the undertaking, *A Calabash of Diamonds*, was published in 1961. The book has a striking black-and-ochre jacket designed by my father, with the title and the author's name, Margaret Lane, spelt out in bones; Russell's map was reproduced as one of the end-papers. *A Calabash* was universally praised by the critics, although several expressed disapproval at the Huntingdons' buccaneering behaviour. Harold Nicolson, for instance, in his review for The *Observer*, referred to my mother as a 'werewolf' whose behaviour had deeply disturbed his Methodist conscience. 'It is (to me) shocking that an educated woman of exceptional talent should conspire with a peer of the realm to rifle a tomb',[33] he wrote. 'They were prepared to evade the passport and Customs regulations of three countries, to steal the hidden heritage of a Zulu tribe, to violate the laws regarding treasure trove, to traffic in illicit diamonds, to smuggle and to lie damnably to Civil Servants, District Commissioners, Game Wardens, and even missionaries.'

My parents' expedition had strangely little impact on the lives of my sister and myself. I remember them setting off for Southampton where they were to board a Union Castle ship to Cape Town, the gossip columnists successfully misled into reporting the departure of the Earl and Countess of Huntingdon on safari in South Africa. In Cape Town they were joined by Peter Cameron, the 39-year-old son of Jack's sister, Marian, and the initial plan was that if the treasure were found, my mother and Peter should quietly return home while my father went to Antwerp to sell the diamonds. 'We knew enough of the law of treasure trove,'[34] my mother wrote blithely, 'to be pretty certain that … whatever we did with it was bound to be illegal.' In the event, and after some alarming adventures en route, they succeeded in reaching the burial ground and setting up camp on what was clearly a sacred site. As they started to dig, 'an ominous drumming' began, and they were warned to leave at once if they wanted to save their lives.

At the time of the book's publication I remember one of my teachers at school remarking how odd she thought it that I had said nothing about what my parents had been up to: most children wouldn't have been able to resist talking about such an adventure, she said. But it had never occurred to me: they were my parents, it was the sort of thing they did, and anyway it had little to do with the far more pressing concerns of my personal life: a threatened detention for talking in Chemistry and whether or not I would get a white girdle for Gym.

---

[33] *The Observer*, 26.3.61.
[34] *A Calabash of Diamonds*, p. 211.

Jack and Cristina returned to Moorea in October 1929 and, at first, life on the island continued very much as before. In different ways they had both been shaken by the serious rupture in their relationship caused by Jack's love affair, and both found it reassuring to return to the place where they had been happy in the past. During their nearly two-year absence, Russell had taken on the job of keeping an eye on the house, which had been let while the Hastingses were away. As well as the usual minor repairs there was the perennial problem of land crabs, armies of them scuttling up from the beach intent on digging themselves into the wooden floor of the veranda. 'I tried the hot water trick on the crabs with considerable success', Russell reported. 'This is by far the most effective and cheapest means I have yet discovered for keeping the brutes reasonably subdued.' Russell had also maintained the plantation. 'The new coconuts on the upper part of the hill are looking well and most of the hibiscus I put in along the fence line are coming on. With the coffee and vanilla plants you asked me to put in I have had poor luck.' As to the little yacht, *White Heather*, 'she is in good shape, and has just been overhauled again'.

After such a long stay in England, it was to be expected that there would be plenty of news arriving from home. Jack's three sisters kept regularly in touch, the most entertaining letters, as always, coming from Marian, who had finally been received back into the family fold after returning from the Falklands with her husband and son.

Among Jack's men friends, by far the most regular correspondent was Alec Waugh. Despite the customary lack of response – 'You are a rogue Jack and a lazy one not to write to me' – Alec faithfully continued to send news, of his part in a Regency pageant of Maud's, of his brother Evelyn's divorce, and of his own unsatisfactory love-life ('it is many moons since romance tarried upon my pillow'). But uppermost in Alec's mind was still Ruth Morris, the woman whom he had first met on Tahiti three years earlier.

Tahiti in the late 1920s and early 1930s was becoming an increasingly popular destination both for wealthy tourists and for writers and artists looking for an exotic location where they could for a time escape the climate and pressures of home. Among the latter was Robert Gibbings, owner of the Golden Cockerel Press and one of the most admired wood-engravers in England. Gibbings had recently illustrated two books which had won him acclaim on both sides of the Atlantic. 'Next time you give me a job, for God's sake send me to the South Seas – I'm sick of English fogs',[35] Gibbings had written to his publishers, who had obliged by paying for his passage to Tahiti.

One of the results of his visit was an illustrated memoir, *Iorana*, which includes a description of the Hastingses house, Faretaotootoa; Gibbings and his wife had gone there one day while Jack and Cristina were away. 'We did no more than dress & undress in your house when by permission of friend Russell we bathed in your pool',[36] he told Jack. 'I would like to assure you however that we did not destroy the cushions neither did we relieve the literary bundles of their string.'

The 'literary bundles' may well have included the work on which Jack was engaged, together with his friend James Hall. Dark, lean and strikingly handsome, Hall had arrived in Tahiti in 1920 with his compatriot and fellow journalist, Charles Nordhoff. The two had met in France shortly after the war, during which both had been pilots in the famous Escadrille Lafayette, about which they had subsequently written a book.

Their partnership continued on their return to the States, and when *Harper's* Magazine commissioned a series of travel pieces on the South Pacific they came out to Tahiti, Nordhoff to remain on the island for the next 20 years, Hall for the rest of his life. Both now married with children, they continued to work on joint projects, of which by far the most profitable was to be their *Bounty* trilogy, the first, and most successful volume, *Mutiny on the Bounty*, to be published in 1932. Jimmy Hall, meanwhile, had

---

[35] *The Wood Engravings of Robert Gibbings*, Patience Empson (J. M. Dent, 1959).
[36] Robert Gibbings to JH 27.10.32. HRC.

for some time been planning a book about Tahiti, and having read *The Golden Octopus* and being aware of Jack's knowledge of local legends, had suggested a collaboration.

The Hastingses friendship with the Halls and Nordhoffs dated back to their first arrival on the islands, and every month when Jack and Cristina sailed over to Papeete the three couples met, either at the Halls's house ten miles outside town, or with 'Nordy' and his Polynesian wife, Vahine, on the edge of the peninsula. Both Americans were bookish, intelligent and intensely private, Nordy in particular always diving for cover before the arrival of a ship-load of tourists. Jack relished their company and loved the stories they told, particularly about their wartime exploits. In the end, however, the work they planned came to nothing: a play of Jimmy Hall's was suddenly accepted for production requiring his immediate presence in New York. 'About our collaboration project,'[37] he wrote to Jack soon after his departure, 'I haven't been able to do a thing with respect to my share of it … I feel awfully guilty about this.' Jack had little occasion for disappointment, however, as he had already become involved in a new undertaking.

With the enormously increased audiences for the movies, French Oceania in recent years had become a popular location for the film industry. In 1928 MGM in association with the distinguished director, Robert Flaherty, had enjoyed a notable success with *White Shadows in the South Seas*, an adventure story filmed on Tahiti. Jack had seen it and been inspired to explore the possibility of developing a cinema project himself. While in London, he had invested some money in a small film company and was eager to promote the idea of making a picture set in Polynesia. In this he had been encouraged by the actor, Douglas Fairbanks, whom Jack had encountered in Hollywood shortly before returning to England in 1927. 'Let me know when your picture is finished,'[38] Fairbanks had written to him, 'and I shall be

[37] James N. Hall to JH 7.6.30. HRC.
[38] Douglas Fairbanks to JH. HRC.

glad to give instructions that every facility is afforded you for a favourable presentation.'

Jack had been much taken with the charm and easy manner of the world-famous star, who had been equally impressed by meeting him: not only was Fairbanks fascinated by the English upper classes – he counted both the Prince of Wales and the Duke of Kent among his personal acquaintance – but five years earlier, in one of his most celebrated roles, he had played the 'brave Earl of Huntingdon', alias Robin Hood. How could he not be excited to encounter in person Robin Hood's direct descendant? A couple of years later, when the Hastingses were again in California, Fairbanks invited them to the première of *The Gaucho*, his new movie. Doug himself made a speech from the stage, reminding the audience that it was his film *Robin Hood* that had been shown at the opening ceremony of this very theatre. He then paused, and pointing into the auditorium announced dramatically, 'and there sits the direct descendant of Robin Hood himself!' – at which point every spotlight in the building swung its beam on an extremely startled Jack.

Grateful for Fairbanks's interest in his cinematic project, Jack was able to repay the favour: when the actor visited Tahiti, at a time when the Hastingses were absent, he stayed for a while at Faretaotootoa. 'I hear that Douglas is very happy in your house in Moorea,' Jack was told by a neighbour, while other friends, thrilled to have such a glamorous visitor on the island, reported that the swash-buckling Doug had become 'the hostesses'[39] delight … [he] not only carried the full weight of a dinner party with his knife-swallowing and serviette-vanishing legerdemain, but sent back to each and every lady who had entertained him a silver cigarette box, inscribed with his own handwriting'.

What, if anything, happened to the plans Jack discussed with Fairbanks is unknown, but soon afterwards another opportunity arose. In May 1929 Robert Flaherty returned to Tahiti to start

---

[39] *Rainbow in Tahiti*, Caroline Guild (Hammond, Hammond, 1951) p. 196.

work on a new project in association with the great German director, Friedrich Wilhelm Murnau.

Murnau, who had emigrated to Hollywood only three years earlier, was best known for his 1922 film *Nosferatu*, while Flaherty's master-work to date was a documentary about an Inuit family, *Nanook of the North*. Their new film, *Tabu*, recounting the tragic love story of a young pearl fisher and a beautiful maiden sacred to the gods, and thus 'tabu', was beset with difficulties almost from the start. The two film-makers were by temperament complete opposites: Murnau, tall, sandy-haired, was moody, fanatical and remote, while Flaherty was plump, sociable, talkative, and loved to entertain the company on the violin which went with him everywhere. As Jack later remarked, 'I was puzzled how two such divergent points of view as Murnau and Flaherty had decided to make a picture in partnership.'[40]

Trouble had begun even before the first day's shooting when news arrived from the States that the company backing the film had been badly damaged in the Wall Street crash. The extravagant Flaherty was permanently broke, and so it was left to the more frugal Murnau to finance the film himself, and he turned to Jack for help. 'As I had call on some capital from a small film company of which I was a director,'[41] Jack later explained to Flaherty's biographer, 'I decided to join Murnau and got the consent of the other directors to invest the [necessary] cash.'

The main location for the film was the island of Bora-Bora, just over 150 miles from Tahiti, most of the scenes to be shot on a small atoll, known as Motu Tapu, in the main lagoon. Unfortunately, this was considered a sacred site by the islanders, many of whom refused to set foot on it, and from the moment the film crew arrived almost everything went wrong: schooners carrying essential supplies were late or failed to arrive, two cameras and substantial film stock were lost when submerged by

---

[40] *The Innocent Eye: the Life of Robert J. Flaherty*, Arthur Calder-Marshall (W. H. Allen, 1963) p. 127.
[41] Ibid.

a wave, the location's cook died in an accident, the leading lady became pregnant, and most of the crew went down with mumps.

It was nevertheless an intensely interesting experience for the Hastingses, both of whom stayed on the island throughout the filming, sleeping under canvas, rising at dawn to wash in the stream, breakfasting with the cast and crew before crossing to the atoll where the day's work began. Indeed the filming of *Tabu* soon became a popular tourist attraction and a number of visitors came out to the island to watch. Flaherty was constantly being asked to turn his camera on one tourist or another sporting gaily in the surf, and he always politely obliged although, as he later told Jack, without putting any film in the camera. Easily the most distinguished visitor was Henri Matisse, who had arrived in Tahiti in March 1930 and came over to Bora-Bora to watch the final few days' shooting. As might be expected Jack was fascinated to encounter the famous painter in person, and wrote a detailed description to his sister Marian. 'How *thrilling* meeting Matisse!' she replied – but what he said on the subject no longer survives.

Jack made good friends with both Murnau and Flaherty, and more than once found himself acting as peace-maker in the frequent flare-ups between them. He was charmed by the ebullient Bob Flaherty's sense of drama, particularly his accounts of filming *Nanook* above the Arctic Circle. '[I] loved to listen by the hour to his stories,'[42] he said later. 'He related them so vividly that I can still clearly see Flaherty driving his team of huskies with the inevitable violin tied to the top of the load.' Yet it was with the reserved, perfectionist Murnau that he planned to enter a further working relationship. Murnau had so fallen in love with Tahiti that he had built a house on the westernmost tip of the island, where he pressed the Hastingses to stay. '[I] shall be glad to see you both here whatever day next week you may choose,'[43] he told them. 'I have a

---

[42] Ibid
[43] F. W. Murnau to Cristina Hastings 17.5.30. HRC.

little Marquesan guest house – a roof and a very big couch to sleep on. You may decide after you have seen it whether it will do.'

More than that, he made a proposal, which Jack immediately accepted, that the two of them should work together on a film version of Kipling's novel, *Kim*, to be shot the following year in India. Meanwhile, with the location work finished, both Murnau and Flaherty returned to the States for the final editing and eventual première of *Tabu*. However, three days before the film's first showing – on 18 March 1931 – Murnau was killed in a car accident while driving along the Californian coast.

Shortly after the film crew left for the States Jack and Cristina returned to Moorea, preparing to settle back into the comparative quiet of their previous existence, Jack keen to return to his painting. But then suddenly everything changed. Their friends from California, Ruth and Govie Morris, arrived with a present, a wild cat, one of the many that prowled about the island. As Jack's later portrait of her shows, Zupatina was a hefty animal, striped, with a white front and baleful yellow eyes; she was fierce and untameable, and one day when Jack bent down to stroke her she bit him on the thumb.

The wound quickly turned black and by the evening Jack was running a high temperature. By next morning he was delirious, and Cristina was so alarmed she made up her mind to take him over to the main island where he could be seen by a doctor. Unfortunately a high wind was blowing, and it was only when she offered the bribe of a barrel of rum that she managed to persuade a couple of native boatmen to make the stormy crossing to Papeete. Here Jack was examined by old Dr Cassiau, who told him he had blood poisoning and that the wound had turned gangrenous; although by now seriously ill, he would undoubtedly recover, Cassiau reassured him, but to avoid the very real risk of further complications he must leave the tropics as soon as possible.

Although the doctor's words came as a shock, both Jack and Cristina had known they were not going to stay on Moorea for

ever. It would be a wrench to leave – for the rest of his life Jack
looked back on Moorea as his earthly paradise – but both felt
ready to explore further afield, to re-enter a larger world. On 14
October 1930 the Hastingses left Papeete for the last time. The
previous few weeks had been spent in saying their goodbyes and
packing up their belongings before placing the empty house in the
care of Sam Russell. Jack had asked Russell to sell Faretaotootoa as
soon as possible as he knew he would never return.

Arriving in San Francisco, they again spent a few days at the
St Francis Hotel, adjusting to the change of pace, before driving
down the coast to stay with the Morrises in Monterey. Since they
had first met the Morrises with Alec Waugh, the two couples had
become close, and it was Govie who was to have a considerable
influence on Jack's career in California. A great-grandson of one of
the Founding Fathers of the United States, Govie was well-to-do,
a banker as well as a prolific novelist and writer of short stories,
many of which had been adapted for the cinema. He himself had
worked as a screenwriter in Hollywood and knew both Flaherty
and Murnau – it was while driving to see Govie to discuss a book
version of *Tabu* that Murnau had been killed. Like Jack, Govie had
fallen in love with the South Seas, buying a plantation on Tahiti,
and during the Morrises' visits there the two couples spent as
much time as they could together, both on the main island and on
Moorea, Govie and Ruth always arriving at Faretaotootoa laden
with new books and gramophone records. 'You and Jack were
lovely to us',[44] Ruth wrote to Cristina after one of these occasions.
'We miss you all – it was such loads of fun.' Now the Hastingses
were to be the guests of the Morrises at their house on the hillside
overlooking the beautiful Gulf of Monterey.

'The Gulf of Monterey is three-quarters of an exact circle',[45] Jack
wrote, '[providing one of] the finest prospects of the New World
… On one side golden hills rise from the deep blue of the Pacific,

---

[44] Ruth Morris to Cristina Hastings undated. HRC.
[45] HRC.

on the other stunted cypresses stand in dark groups against the lighter green of the grass ... Further round the bay lies the white Spanish house of my friend Govie.' The Morris property was an impressive residence: built as a single-storey stone house, the original structure had been modernised and enlarged; a 40-foot drawing-room had been added and upstairs two large bedroom apartments, as well as adjacent guest quarters, a courtyard, tennis courts, and an extensive garden, the whole enclosed by a high wall inset with tiles from France and Portugal. The house was spacious, comfortable and elegantly furnished, full of books, paintings, old maps and Chinese porcelain, with a big open fireplace in the main living-room.

Govie, bespectacled, with a strong athletic build and head of thick black hair, was a generous and engaging host. A clever, cultured man, gentle and tolerant, he was an exceptionally entertaining raconteur. In the evenings he would sink into the big black Chesterfield in front of the fire, cigarette in one hand, highball in the other, and regale his audience with all the current gossip, political and social, as well as with stories of his own experiences, from his boyhood in New York to his career in Hollywood. Life with the Morrises was a constant revel. There was tennis and golf, picnics and pool parties, with cocktails available 24 hours a day.

Recalling a typical evening Jack wrote, 'All night Mexican musicians played, while more and more guests arrived. Two pretty Chinese servant girls flitted about like purposeful butterflies, handing drinks and sandwiches.'[46] Many of the Morrises' friends were film people, among the regulars Rudolph Valentino, Pola Negri, Buster Keaton and Charlie Chaplin. The Hastingses had come to know Chaplin the year before while staying in Monterey with Frank McComas, when the star had been much taken with Cristina. Now in one of Ruth's letters to Alec from this period, she wrote, '[Charlie] was very enamored of Cristina Hastings.'[47]

---

[46] HRC.
[47] Ruth Morris to Alec Waugh 17.10.32. Alec Waugh collection, HGARC.

Ruth, much younger than her husband, was possessed of an inexhaustible vitality. Despite her small stature and slender frame, she seemed tireless, up for anything, passionately engaged with whatever was the subject of the moment. There was no one like Ruth for making a party go, yet she never needed to dominate, was as happy to listen as to talk. And in spite of her turbulent love-life – Alec was only one of a series of lovers – Ruth had many devoted women friends, Cristina among them. Yet as Alec tactfully phrased it, 'her restlessness had its defects'.[48] Both the Morrises drank heavily, daily downing vast quantities of bootleg gin minimally diluted with ginger ale. 'Nearly everyone drank too much,'[49] Alec recalled, '[but] Ruth drank much too much.' And when she was drunk the quarrels started, her anger always aimed at her husband, who on the whole managed not only to hold his liquor but to remain relatively unperturbed by his wife's attacks. Yet inevitably these scenes were stressful for their friends, and Jack, on several occasions an unwilling witness, was uncomfortably reminded of similar, if less alcoholic, experiences with Cristina.

Govie was keen to persuade Jack to settle permanently in California, even to adopt American citizenship, and during their stay he took both Hastingses on a tour of the State. He drove them through Yosemite to see the giant redwoods, across the deserted gold country around Sonora, over the barren oil lands of the south, shark-fishing off the coast at Santa Barbara, and finally, to Jack's particular pleasure, north to 'the beauty of San Francisco spreading over the hills around her famous bay'.[50]

They also went to Los Angeles, to look round the studios at Culver City, where Chaplin was editing his new movie, *City Lights*. And it was while in Hollywood that they came across an old acquaintance of Govie's, the immensely wealthy, immensely powerful newspaper proprietor, William Randolph Hearst. Hearst, as always accompanied by his mistress, the film actress, Marion

---

[48] *The Early Years of Alec Waugh*, Alec Waugh (Cassell, 1962) p. 281.
[49] Ibid.
[50] HRC.

Davies, immediately issued an invitation for the two couples to spend a few days at San Simeon, his magnificent estate overlooking the coast halfway between Santa Barbara and Monterey.

Staying at San Simeon was an extraordinary experience. Both Hastingses had of course heard of Hearst's private kingdom, the massive castle he had built and filled with priceless treasures brought over from Europe, pictures and tapestries, stained-glass windows, French, Italian and English furniture. With the Morrises they drove through the great iron gates and up a winding mountain road past herds of cattle and exotic animals, zebras, camels, antelope, before finally reaching San Simeon itself, the great fake-medieval concrete castle. Surrounding it were acres of formal gardens with terraces and fountains, marble statues and cypress trees; just out of sight of the house were swimming-pools, tennis courts, stables and a zoo. As they approached the entrance a housekeeper appeared to show them to their luxurious suites where a maid unpacked their bags.

As a host Hearst was courteous but severe; a big man, well uphol-stered and immaculately groomed, he was unmistakably lord of his domain. The household was run with military precision: absolute punctuality was expected at dinner, served by footmen and three butlers in the magnificent Great Hall hung with Renaissance tapestries; alcohol was rigorously rationed, each guest limited to only one cocktail, and anyone found with liquor in his luggage was immediately asked to leave.

Fortunately the ravishingly pretty Marion Davies, a friendly and effervescent hostess, was more than capable of outwitting the formidable Hearst, and Jack was delighted to find himself in a group discreetly ushered into Marion's bedroom where, giggling, she supplied copious quantities of gin poured from hot-water bottles hidden in her bathroom. When it was time to go downstairs again, great concentration was needed to appear sober before their magisterial host, whom they found, upright and unsmiling, waiting to escort them into dinner.

Yet fascinated though he may have been, Jack was also dismayed by Hearst's profligacy and excess, particularly at a time when much of the country was suffering acute economic hardship from the effects of the Depression. He described the extravagance of San Simeon in a letter to Sam Russell, whose reply clearly echoes Jack's increasingly radical views. 'What you say regarding the Hearst establishment is interesting', Russell replied. 'Flamboyant publicity, noise, and ostentatious spending of money seems to be the life blood of those people.'

Much as he had enjoyed his time with the Morrises, Jack was eager to find somewhere to settle, anyway for a while, so that he could return to his painting, for which he had had little time since leaving Moorea. Fortunately, it was exactly at this point that an interesting opportunity arose. Through Govie, the Hastingses had met a wealthy businessman, George Gordon Moore, on whose vast estate in the Carmel Valley was a redwood cabin, a disused mining shack once lived in by Robert Louis Stevenson. This secluded cabin, now available to rent, was halfway up the mountainside, surrounded by forest and with glorious views, in one direction of the Sacramento Valley and in the other towards San Francisco Bay and beyond to the Pacific Ocean.

When Stevenson arrived there in 1880, he had found the cabin in a state of serious decay, a gloomy, decrepit place with the wreckage of the old silver mine surrounding it. 'Not a window-sash remained',[51] Stevenson wrote. 'The door of the lower room was smashed, and one panel hung in splinters … through a chink in the floor, a spray of poison oak had shot up and was handsomely prospering in the interior.' In his day, living conditions were very basic indeed, with doorless portals covered in thick cloth and only a plank set against one wall providing access to the floor above. Fortunately, however, some modest renovation had taken place since then. 'There is no trace now to remind one of the genius who once lived there',[52] Jack wrote. 'My bedroom was the room actually slept in by Stevenson [but] the bed on which he

---

[51] *Silverado Squatters*, Robert Louis Stevenson (Gutenberg, 2013).
[52] HRC.

slept, made of cow-hide, was burnt by one tenant who was afraid of possible germs … A fire place & chimney & kitchen have been added but the whole remains incredibly rustic.'

Both Hastingses were charmed by the place, as they were by their host, George Moore. A man of almost incalculable wealth, Moore was a somewhat mysterious figure. An American citizen, but rumoured to be the illegitimate son of English royalty, he had lived for some years in London, where he was famous for throwing colossally extravagant parties: at one dinner of his at the Ritz the flowers alone were said to have cost over 2,000 dollars. It was during the war that Moore became a figure of considerable influence, largely through his munificent support for the Commander-in-Chief, Sir John French, for whom he not only provided a house in the capital, but put at his disposal millions of dollars for the war effort, thereby, Jack told Alec, 'possibly saving the British from defeat in the first world war'.[53]

In 1924, having returned to the States, Moore bought the 23,000-acre Rancho San Carlos, where he built a 37-room hacienda, with an artificial lake, a polo field and stabling for over 80 horses. Black-haired and burly, a man of atomic energy, 'with the spirit of a bucking bronco',[54] Moore hunted with passion and was an expert polo player, regularly hosting teams from all over the world. As at the Morris house, if on a much bigger and more lavish scale, the entertaining at San Carlos was almost continuous, and despite Prohibition, champagne and bourbon were on tap at all hours for the stream of visitors that came driving up the miles-long private road through the mountains.

Fortunately for Jack's productivity, the cabin in the woods, in which he and Cristina were to stay for most of that winter, was some distance from the Ranch, and he was able to work for long periods undisturbed. He loved the peace and the pine-scented air, the live oaks and towering redwoods, the streams, the

---

[53] JH to Alec Waugh 29.12.79. HGARC.
[54] *Emerald & Nancy*, Daphne Fielding (Eyre & Spottiswoode, 1968) p. 57.

green, sun-lit hills, with little to disturb his concentration except the chirping of crickets or an occasional eagle gliding over the tree-tops. For Cristina, however, in charge of their household routine, the experience was slightly less serene. It was usually she who drove down the long mountain road to buy provisions, and she who supervised their Filipino servant, whose domestic skills, or lack of them, made Jack think nostalgically of the Morrises' efficient Chinese staff. Here in the forest standards were rather different, he told Govie. 'Sometimes the house is clean and the dinner excellent. At other times untidiness remains unchanged and meals arrive which would have delighted the Marx brothers.'[55]

In its remoteness and simplicity the Hastingses daily routine in California was not dissimilar to their way of life on Moorea. In some ways their relative isolation bound them together, and yet underlying it all was the unavoidable fact of Jack's recent infidelity and his expressed wish to separate. This can hardly have made for an entirely tranquil existence, although Jack's genuine sympathy for his wife, their shared experiences, and Cristina's determination to keep the marriage intact ensured their relationship remained fairly steady, at least for the present. Both intensely private, they never when in company gave the least indication that all was not well between them. As to their little daughter, there were occasional reports of her progress on the other side of the world, from Maud at Burton, and also from Jack's sister Norah, who kept a kindly eye on her two-year-old niece. 'Tell Cristina,' Norah wrote from Northern Ireland, 'Moorea is coming to stay at the sea with my two children. Eleanor & Hyacinth went mad with delight at the mere idea as they *adore* Moorea.'

Meanwhile life in California continued most agreeably. Jack, having completed a fresco for George Moore in the hacienda, was now devoting hours a day to his own painting, invigorated by the fact that Govie had promised to arrange an exhibition for him in San Francisco. And as when staying with the Morrises, the

---

[55] HRC.

Hastingses enjoyed a varied and colourful social life: not only were there parties and polo on George Moore's ranch but also in reach was an unusually interesting community of artists and writers.

Among those whom the Hastingses came to know was the campaigning left-wing journalist, Lincoln Steffens, whose famous statement about the Soviet Union – 'I have seen the future and it works' – is frequently quoted today; Steffens's equally remarkable wife, Ella Winter; Ralph Stackpole, the distinguished sculptor; the rich and eccentric Mabel Dodge Luhan, known for her embattled friendship with D. H. Lawrence; and Erskine Scott Wood, writer, painter, political philosopher, and his long-term companion, Sarah Bard Field. It was with this remarkable couple that the Hastingses formed a particular friendship, on several occasions staying on Wood's beautiful property, Los Gatos, overlooking the Santa Clara Valley.

Born in 1852, Erskine Wood was nearly 80 when the Hastingses met him, much older than Sarah, whom, after the death of his first wife, he was shortly to marry. With his long white hair and bushy white beard, he had the appearance of an Old Testament prophet, a misleading impression for Erskine was left-wing and anarchical, an outspoken free-thinker, famous for his satirical work, *Heavenly Discourse*, which included essays entitled 'Is God a Jew?' and 'The Stupid Cannot Enter Heaven'. A dedicated campaigner for civil liberties, Erskine was a man of impressive intellect and unwavering conviction, admired by both communist intellectuals and well-to-do liberal progressives. Jack immediately fell under his spell, and during the Hastingses visits to Los Gatos spent many hours sitting under a vine-covered pergola on the terrace listening enthralled to his host, Erskine invariably dressed in tunic, baggy trousers and open sandals, his blue eyes alight with passionate enthusiasm.

Sarah, white-haired and beautiful, was also a remarkable personality, a poet and suffragist, loved for her gentleness and acute intelligence, admired by a wide circle of friends. The Hastingses became very fond of her, but inevitably over the years lost touch, mainly due to Jack's apathy as a correspondent. He did contact her, however, after Erskine died in 1944. '[I] liked and admired him so much', he wrote. 'He still remains one of the most vivid personalities I met in America.'

Interestingly it is Sarah's reply to this letter that provides a rare picture of Jack and Cristina. Recalling their visits to Los Gatos, she wrote,

> So many memories of you crowd into my mind: the charm and simplicity of you both, the vividness of your first wife's personality, the delight in finding we not only shared a love of the arts but also liberal political views. I remember, on one of your visits here, your wife was so delighted with a rich crushed strawberry velvet gown of Persian design and make that she insisted on wearing it in the patio though the day was warm and the robe heavy. Then finding her modern English shoes were not in harmony with her costume she took them off and went about barefooted to my husband's and my glee. And I remember, too, how you both came to a Liberal Forum meeting at which my husband and I both spoke and how touched and pleased we were to see you there and to visit with you afterward … Near me, as I write, is the exquisite little Cambodian head you two sent us before taking your bright presences out of reach … Having been writers and, in my husband's case a patron of the arts, many people came to us from all over the world with letters etc. but few ever left such indelible marks behind on both mind and heart as you and your dear Cristina.[56]

Another correspondent who provides a glimpse of Jack and Cristina in California is Una Jeffers, wife of the distinguished poet Robinson Jeffers. The Jefferses were also part of the Los Gatos circle and it was probably there that the two couples met, Una referring to the Hastingses as a pair 'whom we see often and find great dears'.[57] Jack was 'a *nice* Englishman … awfully decent

[56] Sarah Bard Field to JH. HRC.
[57] Una Jeffers to Sara Bard Field 11.10.31. *The Collected Letters of Robinson Jeffers Vol 2 1931–1932*, James Karman (ed.) (Stanford University, 2011).

and full of amusing adventures',[58] while Cristina was approvingly described as 'very dark & dashing'.[59] The Jefferses lived at Tor House, a windswept granite cottage overlooking the sea which they had built themselves. Here Una fiercely protected her husband's privacy, keeping him to an inflexible regime of writing all morning and strenuous physical labour in the afternoon, hanging a wooden sign on the gate, 'Not At Home till 4.0 pm', to discourage visitors. While Robin was physically awkward and painfully shy, Una was small, lively and inexhaustibly energetic, her entire existence dedicated to protecting and providing for her handsome husband.

Charmed by Una's ebullience, the Hastingses enjoyed spending time at Tor House, where the two couples walked for miles along the rocky coast, discussing everything from literature to politics as well as the characters and histories of the friends they had in common. The Jefferses also visited the Hastingses at their mountain shack, and there is a photograph of Robin and Una with Jack and Cristina, all four working hard digging the ground in front of the cabin. Perhaps referring to this occasion, Una in a letter to Sarah Bard Field writes of the Hastingses' 'wee old house up a canon off the Carmel Valley ... with five chairs and a table – (and a Filipino cook who can roast a duck admirably)'.[60]

In many ways the world into which Jack and Cristina had been introduced in California must have seemed almost ideal: most of their friends, Govie, George Moore, the Jefferses, the Lincoln Steffenses, Sarah and Erskine Scott Wood, were remarkable people, highly cultured and intelligent, most of them wealthy, living in the greatest luxury and comfort. And yet most of the group were far from reactionary, the majority liberal, committed to reform, to social equality and civil liberties. Jack, who had long been in rebellion against his own right-wing background, took great inspiration from the enlightened attitudes of these exceptional

---

[58] Una Jeffers to Hazel Pinkham 2.2.31. Ibid
[59] Una Jeffers to Isabelle Call October 1937. Ibid
[60] Una Jeffers to Sara Bard Field 11.10.31. Ibid

personalities, whose views were to influence him for the rest of his life.

At the same time and inevitably he was shocked by what he saw of the beginnings of the Great Depression, the result of the collapse of the American stock market in October 1929. Although the crash had been followed by a brief hiatus when catastrophe seemed to have been averted – 'We have now passed the worst', declared Herbert Hoover in May 1930 – many businesses had been affected, and already there were signs of the devastation to come, shops and houses boarded up, breadlines on the street, and makeshift campsites on the outskirts of town housing migrant families in search of work. Jack was particularly haunted by the grotesque phenomenon of dance marathons, where for weeks at a time before a paying audience desperate couples danced 24 hours a day, permitted only brief hourly breaks and with meals consumed on the move, in the hope of winning a cash prize.

Over the next couple of years there were to be serious conse-quences for some of Jack's closest friends. Within an alarmingly short period both Govie Morris and George Moore were to be faced with ruin, Moore losing almost everything – eight million dollars in one month – including the San Carlos Ranch, while Govie, whose financial stability had been precarious for some time, faced bankruptcy. Typically, he maintained his optimistic outlook, writing to Jack in 1932, 'When I have had plenty of money I have been amused with life. Now that I have none, I am still most enormously amused.'[61] His equanimity and optimism were to be severely challenged, however: his fine house was lost to foreclosure, and he and Ruth eventually ended up living in a small community in the New Mexico desert; here in 1939 Ruth, at the age of 41, eventually drank herself to death, her much older husband surviving her by another 14 years.

It was George Moore who broke the news of the demise in 1953 of 'Poor Govy Morris', by which time the resilient Moore

---

[61] Gouverneur Morris to JH 17.10.32. HRC.

was well on the way to recovery. 'I have hit the jackpot again,'[62] he wrote from his large office in Los Angeles. 'In the Mojave Desert in the past ten years I have developed what is probably the largest deposit of tungsten & gold in the U.S. ...'

In the winter of 1930, however, these cataclysmic events were still in the future. At the beginning of November Jack and Cristina left their cabin in the mountains and once again returned to stay with the Morrises at Monterey. Govie had arranged for Jack to have an exhibition at the Gump Gallery in the famous store of that name in San Francisco. For decades Gump's had been importing art and antiques from the Far East to sell to California's millionaires, and their gallery, if small, had featured some prestigious local painters.

Now for the first time Jack's work, 25 oils, including some numinous paintings of tropical vegetation, a couple of sensuous Tahitian portraits and a number of drawings and water-colours, was to be seen by the public. On the morning of his opening he was gratified to read in the local paper a few lines recommending the show. Yet it was a much lengthier item on the same page that most intrigued him, an announcement of an exhibition at the California Palace of the Legion of Honor of the famous Mexican artist, Diego Rivera. Illustrating the piece was a photograph of one of Rivera's paintings, a portrait of a child. 'I was immediately attracted by this picture,'[63] Jack later recalled, 'and lost no time in going to see the original. The whole exhibition left me exhausted and amazed.'

Uncharacteristically, for Jack was by nature retiring, he determined somehow to obtain a personal introduction to Rivera. It was a meeting that was to change his life.

---

62 George Moore to JH 15.12.61. HRC.
63 JH unpublished ms, HRC.

7

'What circus are you people with?'

The arrival of Diego Rivera in San Francisco, on his first ever visit to the United States, gave rise to considerable excitement. At 42 Rivera was famous throughout the Americas and beyond, officially recognised in his own country as the greatest mural painter of his generation. Much of his early life had been spent abroad, but after years of study in France and Spain, Rivera had returned to Mexico to become involved in a massive government-sponsored mural programme; here his most recent undertaking had been a series of paintings for the National Palace in Mexico City, the most prestigious site for fresco in the country.

Although a prominent and committed communist – in 1927 he had been guest of honour at the 10th anniversary of the October Revolution in Moscow – Rivera's relationship with the Mexican Communist Party had long been embattled: expelled in 1924, he was reinstated in 1926, only to be expelled again in 1929. On this last occasion his relations with the Party had become strained to breaking point after the enormously enthusiastic reaction to his painting in a show in New York, largely funded by that arch-capitalist, John D. Rockefeller.

As a notorious Red, who had mercilessly pilloried American materialism in his murals, Rivera was regarded with suspicion by the United States government, and had been granted a visa only through the personal intervention of the American ambassador to Mexico, Dwight Morrow, who was a fervent admirer of his work. Now, in November 1930, here he was in San Francisco, personally attending the opening of his exhibition – his first major retrospective – at the Palace of the Legion of Honor. The exhibition was not the main reason for his presence, however: Rivera had won an important commission to execute a mural in the newly built San Francisco Stock Exchange.

It was the announcement of this project that had ignited a furore in the press, with half the commentary applauding the commission, the other half angrily condemning it. Among the decriers, local artists were particularly vociferous, resentful that a foreigner should have been brought in to undertake highly paid work that they badly needed for themselves. A more widespread objection was political: was it not a disgrace that an overt revolutionary, a proclaimed Bolshevik who had publicly caricatured American financial institutions, should be invited to work within the sacred portals of the Stock Exchange, that bastion of capitalist economy? 'A storm unprecedented in recent years is shaking the art colony to its very foundations,'[64] one article began. 'The Stock Exchange could look the world over without finding a man more inappropriate for the part than Rivera'.

Yet it was not only Rivera's fame as an artist and his Marxist politics that attracted attention: he himself was a mesmerising personality. Possessed of enormous charm, he was clever, amusing and, despite his massive bulk and dishevelled appearance, imbued with a powerful sexual magnetism. Patronisingly described in one paper as 'a jovial, big-jowled "paisano",[65] Rivera was a figure both fascinating and slightly mysterious, bonhomous and easy to approach, yet curiously detached, as though existing inwardly on a different plane. From the moment of his arrival, he was treated as a major celebrity, besieged by requests for interviews, deluged with invitations from cultural and society figures keenly competing for his presence. 'We were welcomed magnificently by the people of San Francisco,'[66] he recalled, 'and were feted at parties, dinners, and receptions. I received assignments to lecture at handsome fees'. As Rivera's English was minimal, he spoke either in Spanish

---

[64] *United Press*, 23.9.30.
[65] *San Francisco Chronicle*, 11.11.30.
[66] *My Art, My Life*, Diego Rivera with Gladys March (Citadel, 1960) p. 175.

or French, his lectures relayed by an interpreter. Away from the platform, however, he had no need of such assistance as he had an excellent linguist always by his side: his wife, Frida Kahlo.

At 22 Frida Kahlo, Rivera's third wife, was 20 years younger than her husband, to whom she had been married for just over a year. They made a striking pair, Rivera tall and fat-bellied, with bulging eyes and head of thick, unruly black hair, while Frida was tiny, an exquisite little figure in high heels and brightly coloured peasant costume, her dark hair neatly plaited and pinned, like a brittle and beautiful Mexican doll.

This was the couple whom Jack first set eyes on when he attended Rivera's exhibition on 15 November 1930. As usual the artist himself was surrounded by a crowd, and Jack concentrated on examining the paintings, which astonished him. 'Here at last was a painter who had been through all the phases – academic, post-impressionist, cubist – and now had emerged from the laboratory with the power of expressing himself and the world about him in such a way as could appeal to all classes and kinds of people',[67] Jack later wrote in an article. 'It seemed that he had solved the problem, as only the greatest painters have succeeded in doing, of representing understandably and truthfully the outside world, and at the same time creating a source of aesthetic pleasure in the pure form, colour and line of the design.' Determined to meet Rivera, Jack obtained an introduction from Ralph Stackpole, the distinguished sculptor and an old colleague of Rivera's, whom the Hastingses had come to know through Erskine Scott Wood at Los Gatos. It was Stackpole who had initiated the plan to bring Rivera to San Francisco, and it was at Stackpole's spacious studio in the old artists' quarter of the city that Diego and Frida were staying.

As Jack made his way to 716 Montgomery Street, apprehensive and excited, he had little idea what to expect. 'The door was

---

[67] JH unpublished ms, HRC.

opened by a small, dark-haired and lovely Mexican woman,'[68] he recalled.

> This was Frida Kahlo Rivera, an extremely gifted and charming person. I asked if Senor Rivera were at home, and she graciously motioned me to come inside. The first thing I saw was an immense unfinished charcoal design covering the whole wall. I realised from the power and beauty of this design, that here at last I had found a vital art, and one truly expressive of today. It was some moments before I recollected myself enough to greet Senor Rivera, who was watching me with a smile across a long draughtsman's table at which he was working on further designs.

As the two men talked, in French, as Jack had little Spanish, Jack felt himself spellbound, almost as fascinated by the artist's appearance and manner as by his speech. 'Rivera is tall and fat. He has small feet and remarkably neat little hands. His eyes protrude, and he seems able to look sideways without turning his head. He has great charm, a keen sense of humour and astounding intelligence.'[69] After half an hour or so of general conversation, Jack summoned the courage to put the crucial question. 'I asked Rivera if he would accept me as one of his assistants. He agreed, and the next day I began the routine of apprenticeship.'

It remains something of a mystery why an artist of Rivera's standing should have been willing to take on this completely unknown Englishman. By this stage in his career, Rivera was frequently petitioned by eager young artists begging to work with him, of whom most were courteously turned away, so what was so appealing about Jack? Rivera had no ties to England, and with his political affiliations was unlikely to have been impressed by titles or ancestry. Presumably Jack had brought a small portfolio to show him, but it is difficult to believe that these early efforts would have been regarded as particularly impressive. Perhaps Rivera was

---

[68] Ibid.
[69] Ibid.

amused by the unlikeliness of the situation, even touched by the young man's passionate enthusiasm, or perhaps it was simply that he trusted his old friend Stackpole's judgement.

The following morning Jack began work. He and Cristina were staying at the newly built Gaylord Hotel on Jones Street, a half-hour's walk from the studio. Here on Montgomery Street, up a dark staircase on the third floor, Jack arrived to find a scene of intensely social industriousness, a group of people variously employed in a large airy room, 'crowded with glass jars of paint, tacked canvases, a Spanish guitar, rolls of drawings and plans and all the clutter of an artist'.[70]

There was a large table in the centre, with to one side a big double bed, a broken-down old sofa and several rickety wooden chairs; Rivera, who had hung full-sized cartoons on the walls, was perched on a ladder painting with great concentration, brush in one hand, a china plate for his palette in the other. Around him, busy and absorbed, were his three assistants, the surrealist painter Matthew Barnes, employed as plasterer, Albert Barrows, an engineer, helping with technical advice, and Clifford Wight, an English sculptor who had worked previously with Stackpole and studied under Rivera in Mexico. As well as acting as supervisor, Stackpole himself was working on designs for a group of figures for the outside of the Stock Exchange building. He and his wife Ginette lived in the studio, which served not only as a place of work but as a centre for the local artists' community, many of whom dropped in during the day to chat and to watch what was going on.

Away from the others, sitting quietly in the background, was the artist's wife. Frida, in a long silk skirt, her bare feet in Mexican sandals, spent much of the day at her easel, cheerfully singing to herself, now and again darting across the room to put her arms round Diego and give him a kiss on the back of his neck. At lunchtime she and Ginette Stackpole prepared food for the team, making sandwiches or scrambling eggs over the one gas burner,

---

[70] Ibid.

and planning the necessary shopping and other errands to be carried out the following day. Inevitably, with their husbands so intensively occupied, the wives spent much time in each other's company, and it was during this period that a warm friendship between Frida and Cristina evolved.

Once Jack had departed for his day's work, Cristina was left to her own devices. By now the Hastingses had spent enough time in California to have made a number of friends, and Cristina had plenty of society, other women with whom to lunch and go shopping, and couples such as the Morrises and Jefferses with whom she could spend the day. And yet she preferred to pass most of her time in the studio, fascinated by watching the work in progress, while also wanting to keep an eye on Jack. In this she and Frida had a common bond: both with husbands who were susceptible to other women. They shared, too, a sense of foreignness, Cristina much entertained by Frida's dislike of America, which she referred to as 'Gringolandia', and by her wicked mockery of the wealthy socialites competing to entertain Rivera; these 'gringo people',[71] as she called them, 'are very dull and they all have faces like uncooked bread.'

For the past couple of years Frida had been a member of the Communist Party and, more than her anti-Americanism, it was her left-wing politics that had a powerful appeal for Cristina. Frida, for her part, was sympathetic to Cristina's sense of displacement, her wild mood swings between boredom, humour and explosive anger. The two of them had a keen interest in fashion and style, Frida admiring Cristina's Italian chic while Cristina was intrigued by Frida's highly personal interpretation of traditional Mexican costume. It was during this period of their early friendship that Frida drew a pencil portrait of Cristina, movingly conveying an underlying sadness as well as her subject's sophistication and hauteur.

---

[71] *The Letters of Frida Kahlo: Cartas Apasionadas*, Compiled by Martha Zamora (Chronicle Books, 1995) p. 108.

As the two couples came to know each other, they began to spend more time together outside the studio. There were a number of good restaurants near Montgomery Street, where the four of them often dined together, usually joined by colleagues of Rivera's or by friends of Jack's, such as the Morrises and Jefferses. On a number of occasions the Hastingses accompanied the Riveras on their exploratory expeditions in the city. Diego, overwhelmed by the natural splendour and material wealth of California, was fascinated by San Francisco, its magnificent buildings and broad boulevards, its docks and wharves, cable cars and department stores, regarding it as one of the most beautiful cities in the world.

The Riveras as they walked the streets naturally attracted a good deal of attention, 'the gargantuan Mexicano,'[72] with his ten-gallon hat and big cigar, accompanied by the dazzling, doll-like figure of his wife in elaborately embroidered costume and heavy jewellery, her hair braided with bright woollen ribbons and studded with blossom. One evening when the four of them were on the Oakland Bay ferry, Jack burst out laughing when a stranger who had been staring at their little group came over to them. 'Say,' he asked, 'what circus are you people with?'[73]

Rivera, eager to gather material for his painting, was anxious to see as much as he could not only of the city but of the rest of the state, and it was on these expeditions that Jack, fluent in French after two years in the South Pacific, was delegated to act as interpreter. In the Hastingses' car, with Jack and Cristina taking turns at the wheel, the two couples set off for a tour of the surrounding country.

For the young Englishman it was a memorable experience, and he was enthralled not only by the places they visited but by the artist's extraordinary powers of observation. 'We visited farms and mines, docks and factories, and even the observatory of Mount Hamilton, where we were allowed to operate the giant telescope

---

[72] *San Francisco News*, 7.7.34.
[73] *The Mexican Muralists in the United States*, Laurance P. Hurlburt (University of New Mexico Press, 1989) p. 100.

and observe the moons of Uranus. Wherever he went Rivera's pencil would be noting what he saw, and I would be translating the innumerable questions from that mind which never grew tired.'[74]

Returned to Montgomery Street, Jack continued in the same role, an essential intermediary between Rivera and the multitude of visitors who dropped in throughout the day. 'In this way,'[75] Jack recalled,

> I took part in innumerable discussions between Rivera and artists, architects, art patrons, professors, politicians, business men, actors and engineers, for a never ending stream of people called at his studio, creating interruptions which seriously interfered with his work ... Rivera would often continue the discussion far into the night, and seemed to have an amazing grasp of almost every subject, from hydraulics to religion, from ballet dancing to biology.

Jack recalled one conversation that took place in 'this clearing-house of conflicting opinions': a famous architect was arguing that in the United States it was impossible to interest the general public in art; Rivera replied that the reason for the public's indifference was the failure of artists to produce work of a quality which could possibly interest them.

With Rivera inundated by invitations to give talks and to attend social events, it was also part of his new assistant's job to take charge of his employer's diary, a responsibility that presented considerable problems of its own. '[I] had to arrange a timetable, and, most difficult of all, try to make Rivera keep his appoint-ments, for the ideas of punctuality prevailing in Mexico and the United States seemed to differ by some hours.'[76] Diego was often asked to lecture, amiably agreeing, and then forgetting all about it

---

[74] JH unpublished ms, HRC.
[75] Ibid.
[76] Ibid.

until the day arrived when he would explode and pretend he knew
nothing about it.

'The same old Diego,'[77] Clifford Wight wrote sympathetically to
Jack after one such occasion. '[He] accepts most graciously at first
and then tries to get out of it after the announcements and invitations have been made and then says how *emmerdant* these people
are and gets mad.'

One of the many callers at Montgomery Street was the famous,
and very beautiful, tennis champion, Helen Wills. In her memoirs
Helen Wills describes her first visit to the studio, 'where a number
of artists and helpers were working ... A great cartoon on paper
of the Stock Exchange fresco hung on one wall ... And Diego
Rivera was everywhere, drawing, directing, planning, talking.
Lord Hastings was being sent out as messenger boy to buy some
drawing paper, and I met him in the doorway. They seemed to
be having fun.'[78] Diego was much taken with the lovely Helen
Wills, herself an amateur artist, and asked if she would sit to him
for the head of the mural's central figure, the Spirit of California.
'He sketched in sanguine chalk before my astonished eyes, on a
colossal scale, while standing on a soap box,'[79] Helen recalled.

However, when members of the Stock Exchange committee
called one day to find that a specific individual was to be
portrayed, they vigorously objected. 'This started all the artists
off on a rampage,'[80] Helen reported, 'and when the committee had
left, Rivera snorted, and Lord Hastings laughed, and the artists
all denounced all stockbrokers.' Determined to have his own way,
Rivera ignored the objections, simply changing the colour of his
subject's hair from blonde to black and leaving the face largely
unaltered. Rivera was pleased with the results, 'greatly intrigued,'[81]
as Jack wrote later, 'to discover that the proportions of her features

---

[77] Clifford Wight to JH 14.12.32. HRC.
[78] *Fifteen Thirty: the Story of a Tennis Player* by Helen Wills (Scribner 1937) p. 183
[79] Ibid.
[80] Ibid.
[81] JH unpublished ms, HRC.

in his profile drawing exactly corresponded to a famous drawing by Leonardo da Vinci'. After Rivera had finished with it, the portrait was bought by Jack, who later presented it to the Tate Gallery in London.

It was Helen Wills who at one remove was partly responsible for the most substantial of Rivera's commissions in the United States. In 1928, while playing in a tennis tournament in Detroit, Helen had met the director of the city's Institute of Arts, the German art historian, William Valentiner. The scholarly Dr Valentiner was bowled over by the beautiful sportswoman and a close, not to say passionate friendship developed between them. ('I am suddenly more interested in tennis than in art',[82] Valentiner confided to his diary. 'My studies remain untouched ...') It was mainly in order to see Helen again that Valentiner visited California in December 1930, and it was through Helen that he met Rivera. The two men talked, Valentiner outlining the possibility of a major project in Detroit, an appealing prospect for Diego, who was anxious to see for himself one of the great industrial centres of America. Before Valentiner left town, he had not only prepared the way for an important commission but had also made plans to mount an exhibition of some of Rivera's work – including the drawing of Helen Wills – at the Detroit Institute.

As recorded in Valentiner's diary, the Hastingses, too, had been present at his initial meeting with Diego. Helen Wills had put herself out to entertain her visiting admirer, organising an elaborate tea-party at her house, preceded by an exhibition game of tennis, to which both the Riveras and the Hastingses were invited. Rivera had never seen tennis before, and Valentiner was intrigued to watch the great man seated in the umpire's stand, mopping his forehead with a large coloured handkerchief and turning his head from side to side, '[like] one of those Chinese pagodas with

---

[82] *The Passionate Eye: the Life of William R. Valentiner*, Margaret Sterne (Wayne State University Press, 1980) p. 186.

rocking tops'.[83] After the game they all went indoors to tea, and among the guests Valentiner particularly noticed two women.

> One was Rivera's wife, Frida, who seemed especially charming … The other woman was Lady Hastings, the daughter of the Marchesa Casati well known from the fantastic, red-haired portrait of her by Augustus John. She and Lord Hastings travelled everywhere with Rivera, which reminded me of the days of the 'Grand Tour' when the English aristocracy were found wherever good art was being produced.[84]

By the middle of December the preliminary studies for the mural were complete, and Diego and his team moved into the Stock Exchange. The space to be covered was a 30-foot wall on the staircase leading up to the Luncheon Club, a spacious, thickly carpeted room, with deep armchairs and an ornate art-moderne décor. The fresco's theme was that of the richness and fertility of the State: at the centre is Calafia, the huge and heroic personification of the Spirit of California, holding in her arms the symbols of her fertility, one hand filled with mineral wealth from below the ground, the other with a copious offering of fruit and vegetables; on either side are figures absorbedly engaged in shipping, in science, engineering, farming, mining, including in the foreground a boy holding an aeroplane, a portrait of Ralph Stackpole's teenage son.

If Jack had found his duties demanding while working in the studio, they were nothing to the relentlessness and long hours experienced once they were on site. After the scaffolding was erected, the assistants, under Clifford Wight's direction, prepared each section in turn, layering the wet plaster onto the wall and tracing on it the designs for Rivera to start painting. As the paint had to be applied before the plaster dried, Rivera, in baggy brown sweater and paint-stained corduroy trousers, regularly worked for 12 and 14 hours at a stretch – on one occasion, when painting the

---

[83] Ibid., p. 188.
[84] Ibid.

figure of a nude Helen Wills on the ceiling, for 23 hours without stopping. He was perfectly happy to talk while he worked, and time and again Jack found himself sitting next to Rivera on the scaffold while the great man talked animatedly about politics and painting.

Jack was enormously impressed by Diego's unflagging energy and powers of concentration. '[Rivera] to a great extent redis-covered the difficult technique of fresco,'[85] Jack wrote later, 'that is painting with colours ground in water on wet plaster. On a large scale this method requires long hours of continuous work, great physical endurance and masterly draftmanship.' Once when the artist was determined to achieve exactly the right blue, Jack watched him repaint the area nine times while his assistants continued to grind cobalt on the floor far below him. For Diego's assistants, Jack recalled, 'Life was very much as I imagine the life of an artist's apprentice in the middle ages must have been ... We had to grind colours, wash brushes, plaster walls, enlarge designs, do odd jobs generally, paint skies and unimportant parts of the background, and so came up against difficulties and problems and saw at first hand how they were solved.'[86]

Astonishingly, the mural was finished in a little under four weeks, by the beginning of February 1931, leaving Rivera himself so exhausted that he gratefully accepted an invitation from a wealthy local patron to stay at her house and recuperate for a month. His next project was to be a mural in the San Francisco School of Fine Arts, but meanwhile, with the master away, the pressure for his assistants was off, and it was during these few weeks that Jack and Clifford Wight spent much of their time together, cementing a friendship that was to last for decades.

Clifford, tall, dark, very good-looking, was only a year older than Jack. Born in England, he had emigrated to Canada as a very young man to join the Mounted Police, before moving to

---

[85] JH unpublished ms, HRC.
[86] Ibid.

Mexico in the early 1920s specifically to work with Rivera. A talented painter and sculptor – and like his mentor a committed communist – Clifford was much relied upon by Diego, who left in his hands all the business of ordering supplies, writing and translating letters, devising timetables, and overseeing the work of his team. A strong personality, Clifford ran a tight ship, but he could also be delightful company, wry, funny and kind-hearted. His one flaw, in the eyes of most of his friends, was his American wife, Jean.

When Jack first met them, Jean and Clifford had not long been married, and Clifford was besotted with the ravishing ex-model, adored her for her tall blonde beauty, and considered her perfect in every aspect. To the others, however, Jean appeared vain, stupid and extremely boring, resented particularly by the wives for her outrageously flirtatious manner with their husbands. Frida, who took a photograph of Jean roguishly ogling a far from unreceptive Diego, was particularly irritated by her. 'Jean has nothing in her head but idiocies',[87] she complained. 'She talks all day of "fashions" and of stupidities that don't amount to anything … in addition she does it with a pretentiousness that leaves one cold.'

With Diego away, Jack, much encouraged by Clifford, set about finding some commissions of his own. An opportunity that immediately attracted him was the announcement of the opening of the World's Fair in Chicago, planned for 1933. Here Jack had a useful contact, his old friend from Oxford, William McGovern, with whom he had once planned an expedition to explore the upper reaches of the Amazon. The two men had kept in touch, and McGovern, now living in Chicago, was more than willing to help, offering to put Jack in touch with Rufus Dawes, the president of the Fair and a personal friend of his. 'It would certainly be most marvellous',[88] he wrote, 'if you could get some work for the World's Fair which would bring you here to Chicago so that I could have

---

[87] *Frida: a Biography of Frida Kahlo*, Hayden Herrera (Harper & Row, 1983) p. 122.
[88] William McGovern to JH 31.3.31. McGovern collection, Northwestern University.

the chance to see you and Cristina once more.' Jack duly applied, sending photographs of some of his South Seas paintings, and to his pleasure and surprise was offered a job for the following year of executing a design for the Fair's Hall of Science.

Meanwhile, there was work nearer to hand, a fresco for his old friend Govie Morris in Monterey. Govie was a great admirer of Rivera's, to whom he had been introduced by Jack. In an article Govie described Rivera as '[a] kind, wise, witty, generous prodigy of a man,'[89] and he bemoaned the fact that there was so little general interest in mural painting in California. Thus Govie was delighted to have a fresco by Jack, and Jack for his part was pleased to be able to repay some of his friend's unfailing kindness, undertaking the job for nothing except the cost of materials. The painting, slightly formal, full of colour and with a bold design, took nearly three months to complete. Govie is seated in the foreground, surrounded by representations of his life and career: a Hollywood cameraman, his wife Ruth flying overhead in her little plane, to one side RMS *Tahiti*, the ship that plied between Papeete and San Francisco, and in the background the house in Monterey, the skylines of San Francisco and New York. Also depicted are two significant references to Tahiti: in one hand Govie holds a miniature female nude, a Gauguinesque *vahine*, a reference to the passion he shared with Jack for the painter; and in the middle of the foreground is the large and menacing figure of Zupatina, the wild cat given to Jack by the Morrises, whose bite resulted in his having to leave the islands.

Diego, meanwhile, had returned from his month away to begin on the new work in the California School of Fine Arts. Jack in Monterey was kept in touch with what was going on by long gossipy letters from Clifford. The subject of Diego's new design, *The Making of a Fresco*, focuses on the actual process of painting the mural: in the middle of the piece is the scaffold, and on it are portraits of the painters at work, all viewed from the rear, the

[89] 'Diego Rivera', Gouverneur Morris, undated article (Syracuse University).

large and corpulent figure of Rivera himself in the centre, with his assistants above, below and beside him. 'By the way, *you* are to be immortalised in fresco tomorrow',[90] Clifford told Jack at the beginning of May – and there indeed he is, at the very top left-hand corner hanging a plumb-line, with Clifford kneeling opposite him on the right.

The painting on which they are all absorbedly engaged is that of the immense figure of an industrial worker in blue overalls and hard hat, to which Diego, typically, was unable to resist a provocative embellishment. 'What do you think the son of a gun has just this minute done?'[91] Clifford wrote delightedly to Jack. 'He has painted the Badge of Communism on the shirt of the worker – the big figure! A red star with the cross & hammer & sickle in yellow. That is going to start something!' And so indeed it did. After the work was unveiled at the end of May there was some shocked reaction not only to the communist insignia but to the fact that the artist had insultingly chosen to portray himself in back-view, his large posterior dominating the very centre of the painting.

By the time such comment appeared in the press, however, Diego had gone, urgently summoned back to Mexico to complete the mural in the National Palace left unfinished the previous year. The Riveras were to stay away for five months, returning to the States in November for an important exhibition of Diego's work in New York. During this time the main link between the two couples was the correspondence between Frida and Cristina, whose warm and emotional friendship continued to flourish. 'I received your beautiful post card',[92] Frida wrote to 'Cristina preciosa' in September.

When I saw it I thort that it is the best portrait of myself; I am sending to you a colection of fonier Mexican post-cards about love and many things ... also, I am very sorry because I couldn't buy for

---

[90] Clifford Wight to JH nd. HRC.
[91] Clifford Wight to JH nd. HRC.
[92] Frida Kahlo to Cristina Hastings 24.11.31. HRC.

you the cigarettes you wanted … Please write me and don't forget mi chica … For you and Jack, *mis mejores recuerdos lo mismo de la parte de Diego*. Besos de Frida[93] … *Don't forget me.*[94]

With this letter she included on a separate piece of paper a lipstick kiss, below it six X's and the words, 'Don't forget me darling, ever.'

It was in a letter from Frida in September that Jack learned to his pleasure that Diego had approved of his fresco for Govie Morris. 'I want to tell you that we liked *very very much* the fresco of Jack,'[95] Frida told Cristina. 'Diego is so busy that he could not write you, *pero estuvo encantado lo vió*[96] He will write later to Jack … Diego says his fresco is really very good.' Diego shared with Jack an extreme reluctance ever to put pen to paper: 'Rivera says he would rather paint two walls than write a letter,'[97] William Valentiner noted in his diary; and at this period it was usually Clifford who drafted his correspondence.

Diego did, however, manage to write to Jack a couple of months later, by which time the Riveras had left Mexico for New York. 'Mon cher ami Jacques,'[98] Diego's letter begins, handwritten in his colloquial French. 'On vous aura dit aussi combien j'ai aimé par la photo, la fresque que vous avez fait pour Monsieur Morris, c'est très jolie … Si vous avez encore un photo envoyez la moi pour la montrer.'[99] The letter continues with an account of his exhibition at the Museum of Modern Art – 'deux milles personnes par jour à l'éxposition beaucoup de succès,'[100] before continuing with more mundane matters, such as the settling of accounts for the Stock Exchange mural. 'Jacques, je vous envoie trois cent dollars ici,

---

[93] '… my fondest memories [and] the same on behalf of Diego. Kisses from Frida …'
[94] Ibid., 2.9.31.
[95] Ibid.
[96] 'but was delighted by what he saw'
[97] *The Passionate Eye*, p. 202.
[98] Diego Rivera to JH nd. HRC.
[99] 'I want to say how much I liked from the photo the fresco you did for Mr Morris, it's very pretty. If you have a photo send it to me so I can show it.'
[100] 'two thousand people a day at the exhibition much success'

faittez [sic] en ce que vous voudrez avec, je sais que ça ne vous servira bien entendu en tout cas ce n'est qu'une petite partie de ce que je vous dois pour le travail à St Francisco ... Votre ami Diego Rivera.'[101]

Frida had expressed the hope that Jack and Cristina would join them in New York, a wish enthusiastically backed up by Clifford – 'I am very thrilled with New York; but I should enjoy it so much more if you were here',[102] he told them. 'Your enthusiasm for everything is so infectious.' He also made a point of reiterating Diego's approval of Jack's painting. 'Diego is far more enthusiastic about your fresco than you probably imagine from what was said in his letters. He simply raved about it to me – and while he might flatter a little in talking to the painter himself, I know he wouldn't do so in talking to me. Congratulations!'[103]

Clifford in New York was being stretched to the limit by the demands Diego was making on him. Yet although badly missing his wife Jean, who for some weeks remained behind in California, he was clearly enjoying himself and sent the Hastingses some lively descriptions of how he was coping in this new environment. 'Dear Jack & Cristina,'[104] he wrote shortly after the Riveras had arrived,

> Diego is living in a suite in the Barbizon Plaza overlooking Central Park. Frida arrived with American clothes, but oy oy! I do wish you or Jean had been here to give her some pointers. However she has reverted to her Mexican dresses of which she complains she has only three. So she is not enjoying New York, the Hotel, or the parties ... [Mrs Rockefeller Jr] gave a dinner in honor of Diego to which many important people & some art critics were invited.
> Up to the last minute Frieda reluctantly consented to attend, but eventually Diego arrived alone because Frieda's shoes hurt her! ...

---

[101] 'Jack, I'm sending you here three hundred dollars, do whatever you like with it, I know very well it won't help much in any case it's only a small part of what I owe you for your work in San Francisco ...'
[102] Clifford Wight to JH 24.11.31. HRC.
[103] Ibid.
[104] Ibid.

I asked Frida why she didn't go & she said 'Naw! I daunt like these reech pipple!'

The Hastingses would thoroughly enjoy themselves in New York, Clifford was certain. 'I do wish that you two were here. You'd have such a thrilling time ... And Mrs J. D. R. Jr might take a fancy to Jack's fresco & give him a commission.' He finally concluded his long letter, 'And now I want to thank you again ever so much for all the many things that you have done for Jean and me, and particularly for the lovely leather jacket, the Book of Romance, and the delicious things to eat on the train ... I gave Frida the box of chocolates that you sent her.'

But any plans Jack may have had to go to New York came to nothing when in December Cristina was taken ill and had to spend nearly two weeks in Stanford Hospital. Here she was looked after by Dr Leo Eloesser, to whom Frida had introduced the Hastingses. Dr Eloesser, a distinguished thoracic surgeon, had been frequently consulted by Frida during the Riveras' stay in San Francisco, and the two had become close friends. Frida's health was always fragile: as a child of six she had contracted polio, which left one leg shorter than the other, and in 1925 she had been horrifically injured in a traffic accident, injuries resulting in no fewer than 35 operations. Fragile, frequently unwell and often in serious pain, Frida had come to trust Dr Eloesser above all others, and it was thus a comfort to Cristina that it was he who took her in charge. Just before Christmas Jack, clearly in cheerful spirits, was able to report to Clifford that his wife had recovered. 'I am so glad that Cristina is better now,'[105] Clifford replied. 'Diego received Jack's letter a few days ago & had me translate it to Frida. They roared over your jokes.'

Before Rivera left California he had agreed plans with Dr Valentiner that, once finished with his obligations in New York, he should undertake a substantial work in the Institute of Arts

---

[105] Clifford Wight to JH and Cristina Hastings 22.12.31. HRC.

in Detroit, to be financed by Edsel Ford, head of the Ford Motor Company. Contracts had been drawn up, and it had been arranged that the artist should bring with him two assistants of his own choosing, Clifford Wight and Jack Hastings. In a letter to Jack, Clifford described the somewhat complex negotiations in which he had engaged with his employer, which finally resulted in Diego agreeing to pay them both wages of seven dollars a day, with the understanding that Clifford, as the senior employee, would be expected to work half-days only – a meaningless concession, as it turned out, given the enormous workload involved. It was not a great deal of money, Clifford admitted, but he urged Jack to accept.

> My chief motive is that I *do* want to see you both again so for heaven's sake don't disappoint me ... Really it is not at all a bad proposition considering the terrible conditions of wages & unemployment and inability of big artists here to make a single dollar, in addition to the many, many letters & visits that Diego receives from competent young artists begging him to take them on as assistants either for the experience alone or for room & meals only. So I do hope you will take these things into consideration & pull stakes for Michigan muy pronto ...[106] Diego says he will pay Jean's fare out, so please bring her with you – I shall die if I don't see her soon.[107]

As Clifford must have known, Jack needed little persuading. He was immensely gratified to have been picked to work again with Rivera, and he was also curious to see more of the States, Detroit in particular, not only a major industrial centre, home of the Ford motor works, but a city that had been exceptionally hard hit by the Depression. As Diego had written to him,

> A Detroit tout va mal [et] la ville et en banqueroute ... En fin Jacques, il paraît que le mauvais temps est venu pour les uns et pour les autres.

---

[106] Clifford Wight to JH 6.3.32. HRC.
[107] Clifford Wight to JH 8.1.32. HRC.

Ca passera peut être. Où ça deviendra tellement mauvais qu'après ça sera mérveilleux pour tout le monde. Moyennant changement général de rôles dans la vaste force qu'est la mérveilleuse vie[108] ... [sic] vous voyez avec la dépression on devient philosophique.[109]

The Hastingses finally left San Francisco, their little Ford crammed with luggage, in March 1932. The long journey driving east across almost the entire width of the country made an indelible impression. America was now experiencing one of the worst periods of the Depression, with nearly 13 million people out of work, and some of the scenes they saw, the frightful poverty, the sheer numbers of the hungry and homeless, were to influence their political thinking for the rest of their lives.

So far California, with its motion picture industry, defence programme and subsidised shipping, had largely been insulated from the worst effects of the economic crisis. But now as they drove across Arizona, Oklahoma, across the Great Plains, up through Kansas, Missouri and north into Illinois and Michigan, the evidence of a cataclysmic disaster was horrifyingly evident. For hundreds of miles the highway was crowded with trucks and ancient open-topped cars, anxious families perched precariously on piles of clothes, cooking utensils, tattered rugs and blankets, all heading west in a desperate search for work. Walking doggedly along the verge were the transients, thousands of destitute single men with no means of support other than begging or theft: in one month alone the Southern Pacific railroad had evicted an estimated 80,000 transients illegally travelling in its boxcars.

Outside most settled communities were shabby shantytowns, known as Hoovervilles; here the migrants were allowed to

---

[108] Diego Rivera to JH 6.1.32. HRC.
[109] 'In Detroit everything's going wrong, the town bankrupt ... So Jack, it seems bad times have arrived for all. Perhaps it will pass. Where it becomes so bad afterwards it will be wonderful for everyone. Through a general change of roles in the great force that is our wonderful life ... you see, with the Depression, one is becoming philosophical.'

construct temporary shelters, many of them quickly deterio-
rating into slums, strewn with garbage and reeking of human
waste. Death from starvation was far from uncommon, and most
children were visibly malnourished, surviving mainly on beans,
rice and balls of fried dough. In later years, when describing these
scenes, Jack used to say that the ultimate irony lay in the fact that
while millions went without food, farmers to maintain prices were
burning wheat and drowning their hogs, gallons of milk were
poured away and shiploads of coffee taken out to sea and sunk.

By the time he arrived in Detroit, Jack, a Liberal during most
of his twenties, had undergone a considerable shift in his political
philosophy. Rivera's communism had made a significant impact
on both the Hastingses, and now they had seen for themselves
the terrible human consequences of the Depression they were
more than ready to identify with the far left. As Jack's old friend
Alec Waugh wrote, 'The effects of the Depression in America had
made them feel that there was something basically wrong with the
contemporary structure of capitalist society.'[110] Unlike Cristina,
Jack was never to take the final step and join the Communist
Party, although he was to come very near it, with his sympathies
during this period of his life veering strongly in that direction.

---

[110] *The Best Wine Last*, p. 54.

8

'That fresco-paintin', aggravatin' Son-of-a-gun Diego!'

Detroit in the early 1930s was a city in dangerous decline. From a small manufacturing town in the last decades of the nineteenth century, Detroit had become a boom town which had almost quadrupled in volume, its population growing from just under half a million in 1910 to nearly two million by the 1920s. This rapid increase in size and prosperity was mainly due to the enormous expansion of the motor industry, an industry established in the city by Henry Ford, whose company was the first to introduce the assembly line and mass production. Ford's newly completed plant at Dearborn, just outside Detroit, was the largest manufacturing complex in the world. Stretching for over a mile along the River Rouge, with its own docks and railroad track, it had employed at its peak a workforce of over 100,000 men. But with the onset of the Depression, sales of automobiles plunged: 1932 saw the worst year yet for the motor industry, with sales only one-fifth of what they had been three years earlier. Large numbers of workers were laid off at Ford, as elsewhere, with devastating results for Detroit, which was to be harder hit by the economic downturn than any other city in America.

In 1918 Henry Ford (mercilessly caricatured by Rivera in his 1926 Mexican mural, 'Wall Street Banquet'), had officially handed over the presidency of the company to his son, Edsel, although behind the scenes he continued to remain very much in control. It was Ford senior who had recently been responsible for dismissing over 30,000 workers, for reducing wages from 33 to 22 dollars a week, and for creating intensely pressured conditions on the factory floor – no talking, no sitting down, and only

15 minutes allowed for lunch. On 7 March 1932, when a large crowd of recently sacked Ford workers marched to the Rouge plant to demand assistance, it was Henry Ford who authorised the firing by police of thousands of live rounds, a strategy which resulted in five deaths and over 60 men seriously injured. It was later rumoured that Ford had deliberately delayed Rivera's arrival to make sure he would not witness the protest.

Edsel Ford was a very different character from his ruthless, puritanical father. Intelligent, gentle and broad-minded, Edsel was passionately interested in the visual arts, and as president of the Arts Commission was one of the most significant benefactors of cultural life in the city's history. His private collection included paintings by Raphael, Van Gogh, Degas and Matisse, and he was a trustee and generous supporter of the Detroit Institute of Arts, a magnificent Beaux-Arts building on Woodward Avenue which had opened in 1927.

The Institute's director, previously at the Metropolitan Museum in New York, was William Valentiner, who over a period of two years had been vigorously campaigning to bring Rivera to Detroit. This was a project which at first he had had some trouble in promoting. 'Please assure Mr Rivera that I am doing all I can to get the Arts Commission here interested in his work,'[111] Valentiner had written to Clifford Wight in February 1931, 'but I must confess … I find that the difficulties are great in this respect, partly on account of the entire lack of understanding of modern art, and partly for political reasons.' There was also the problem of money: the Institute's annual budget had recently been cut from $400,000 a year to $40,000, with numbers of staff made redundant and even Valentiner himself eventually obliged to take eight months unpaid leave. Fortunately, the situation had been saved by Edsel Ford, who had offered to fund not only the whole of Rivera's fee but also the very expensive preparation of the site. Thus Valentiner's goal

---

[111] W. A. Valentiner to Clifford Wight 5.2.31. Syracuse University.

was finally achieved, with Rivera due to arrive from New York at the end of April 1932.

On Rivera's instructions, Clifford Wight had gone on ahead, arriving in Michigan in the first week of March. Here three weeks later he was followed by the Hastingses. 'It's really very nice to know that Cristina and Jack arrived all ready,'[112] Frida wrote to Clifford from New York. 'I am sure that we will have a grand time altogether. Would be very nice if we lived in the same hotel. Don't you think so? ... Please tell Cristina that I want very much that she writes me. Diego and I send our love to them.' Conveniently there was a large apartment hotel, the Wardell, only a couple of minutes' walk from the Institute, where the Hastingses and Riveras could live almost next door to each other. When Diego and Frida arrived in Detroit on 21 April they were met at the station by Dr Valentiner, by Clifford and Jean Wight, and by the Mexican consul, who escorted them to the Wardell, where they were affectionately reunited with the Hastingses.

As a welcoming gesture towards the famous artist, Edsel Ford had arranged a luncheon in Rivera's honour, to take place in the private dining-room in his office at the factory. As well as Diego, he invited his two assistants, Clifford and another guy described somewhat vaguely by Edsel's secretary as 'some titled Englishman descended from whatever peer led the Battle of Hastings.'[113]

Shortly before his guests were due Edsel suddenly panicked, realising he had forgotten that as Rivera's English was minimal he would need an interpreter. Summoning his secretary, Fred Black, he instructed him to telephone down to the factory floor at once, find someone who spoke Spanish and send him upstairs. Black did as he was told, and a young man straight off the assembly line soon appeared, was quickly ushered in and put to sit next to the guest of honour. The lunch passed without incident, and it was only afterwards it was discovered who the young man was:

---

[112] Frida Kahlo to Clifford Wight 12.4.32. Detroit Institute of Arts.
[113] Fred L. Black 10.3.51. Oral history, Detroit Institute of Arts.

none other than Prince Louis Ferdinand, grandson of the Kaiser. As Fred Black later put it, 'It struck me as kind of a humorous situation to have Diego Rivera ... a communist, who didn't believe in royalty at all, sitting at the same table and being interpreted by the Kaiser's grandson.'[114]

Rivera had been given complete freedom to choose his subject, and he spent nearly three months exploring Detroit, occasionally accompanied by Jack or one of the other assistants. Fascinated by technology, he spent much of his time at the vast Ford complex. 'I studied industrial scenes by night as well as by day,'[115] Rivera recalled, 'making literally thousands of sketches of towering blast furnaces, serpentine conveyor belts, impressive scientific laboratories, busy assembling rooms ... and of the men who worked them all ... I was afire with enthusiasm.' This enthusiasm translated into an astonishing sequence of designs representing the city's indigenous industrial culture, with particular focus on the men and machinery at the Rouge plant. Little escaped him, and as his frescoes were to convey, he had understood very clearly the harsh physical restrictions imposed on the men at the Rouge, the atmosphere of sullen depression on the factory floor.

While Rivera was engaged in his researches, his team, under Clifford's direction, was busy preparing the site: the spacious two-storey Garden Court on the first floor of the Institute of Arts. Approached up a wide flight of stairs leading from the Great Hall, the Garden Court is a lofty baroque fantasy in white marble, a neo-classical temple roofed in glass and lavishly decorated with a complex pattern of arches, grille-work, Doric pilasters and relief plaques of Etruscan motifs, with at the centre a big stepped fountain, described by Diego when he saw it as 'horrorosa'. Around the fountain were dainty arrangements of foliage, with ferns and miniature palm trees planted out as in an Edwardian conservatory, their removal much resented by certain sections of

[114] Ibid.
[115] *My Art*, p. 183.

society. 'Beautiful, well-dressed ladies complained about the loss of their peaceful, lovely garden, which had been like an oasis in the industrial desert of Detroit',[116] Rivera recalled. 'Thanks to me, their charming sanctum was now an epitome of everything that made noise and smoke and dust.'

In a documentary film shot at the time, there is a short sequence set in this dusty building-site of the Garden Court, showing Jack and Clifford lined up with Dr Valentiner and Rivera. Rivera, the scaffold behind him, is in overalls, the three others in tidy suits and ties. Clifford, his hands in his pockets, looks straight at the camera, wholly at ease, while Jack, who hated being filmed or photographed, is fidgeting nervously. In order to give himself something to do, he fumbles in his pocket for a packet of cigarettes, which he then offers to Clifford, before the camera, to his evident relief, moves to focus on Diego and Dr Valentiner absorbed in talk.

The theme of the murals, now widely regarded as Rivera's finest work, centres on the industrial process of manufacture at the Rouge plant. The two vast central panels, crowded with machinery, with lines of workers under unrelenting pressure, show in meticulous detail over 50 separate processes: the assembly lines, the foundry, the furnaces, every stage in the construction of the engine, transmission and bodywork of a motor car. In 25 smaller frescoes are depicted the raw materials produced in the State of Michigan, from mining to farming, as well as the whole range of scientific progress, from geology to surgical operations. In one panel, soon to become notorious, Rivera painted a scene of a baby held by a nurse while being vaccinated by a doctor; the trio is surrounded by a horse, an ox and several sheep, all animals from which the serum is drawn.

Provocatively, Rivera had arranged the three figures to resemble the Holy Family, the Christ-like child's blond hair appearing as a halo, the animals standing as though around a manger, with in

---

[116] Ibid., p. 194.

the background, like biblical Magi, three scientists engaged in an experiment. The row that had erupted in San Francisco over his painting in of a red star on the figure of the worker in the Fine Arts mural had been greatly relished by Diego: but it was nothing compared to the fury expressed when this particular panel in the Garden Court was finally unveiled.

With such a vast expanse to be covered, several new helpers had been taken on, most of them, unlike Jack and Clifford, to work without salary. 'Rivera paid very little, if anything, to his assistants,'[117] one of them explained. 'He probably had 15, 20 letters on some days from all over the globe, from people who wanted to come and work for nothing.' Among the successful applicants were Arthur Niendorf, an ex-Hollywood song-writer; Andres Sanchez Flores, a Mexican who had worked as a chemist at Ford; Stephen Dimitroff, a young Bulgarian art student employed as plasterer; and Ernst Halberstadt, a general handyman also in charge of erecting and maintaining the scaffold. These were joined at the end of May by the only woman in the group, Lucienne Bloch, a painter and sculptor, daughter of the Swiss composer Ernst Bloch.

Still in her early twenties, Lucienne, who spoke excellent French, had met Rivera at a dinner party in New York; a feisty and attractive young woman, she had boldly asked him for a job; indeed she had been so animated and flirtatious that Frida had come up to her afterwards and said, 'I hate you!' Luckily, she had then burst out laughing, and from that moment the three had become friends, with Lucienne even moving in for a time to live with Diego and Frida in their large apartment at the Wardell.

While Rivera was exploring the city, his assistants under Clifford's experienced direction were busy preparing the site, ordering supplies, grinding colours, mixing plaster, cutting stone, and erecting the scaffold. In an extraordinarily short time, less

---

[117] *Diego Rivera: the Detroit Industry Murals*, Linda Bank Downs (Detroit Institute of Arts & Norton, 1999) p. 51.

than four weeks, Rivera announced he was ready to show his drawings for the two main walls of the Garden Court. To celebrate this important occasion, Jack and Cristina invited the Riveras, with Edsel Ford and Dr Valentiner, to their modest one-room apartment, Cristina cooking dinner in the tiny kitchen. 'It was a gay party,'[118] Valentiner recalled, 'except for Rivera's silence, which was probably due to his inability still to follow a conversation in English … That evening he spoke Spanish with Frida, Italian with Lady Hastings, and French with me.' After dinner, Rivera unrolled the two large studies, his theme the evolution of technology as seen through the industrial life of Detroit. Both Ford and Valentiner examined the cartoons with great concentration; both were overwhelmed, 'carried away by the accurate rendering of machinery in motion and by the clearness of the composition.'[119] Indeed, Edsel Ford was so excited that he instantly doubled Rivera's fee, from $10,000 to just over $20,000. It was shortly after this agreeable evening that Dr Valentiner left for Europe, forced to take temporary leave as the Institute could no longer afford to pay his salary.

Rivera began painting in the Garden Court towards the end of May, and as in California the work was demanding and the hours very long. For Jack his chief duties were enlarging Rivera's original cartoons, helping Clifford in covering sections of wall in plaster, and in pouncing the sketches, a technique of transferring the sketch through the paper onto the wall. After Lucienne Bloch arrived from New York, it was Jack who instructed her in this process, rather against Clifford's wishes as he disapproved of women working on site. Resentful of this anti-feminist stance, Lucienne never took to Clifford, although she became devoted to Jack. 'He is always dans la lune,'[120] she wrote in her diary, 'but *so* gentle.'

Once the plaster was applied, Rivera had between eight and sixteen hours to paint before it set. As always, Diego's hours were

---

[118] *The Passionate Eye*, p. 188.
[119] Ibid.
[120] Lucienne Bloch diaries. Detroit Institute of Arts.

extremely irregular: sometimes he arrived in the morning, at other times not appearing till late at night, when he would start first on completing the preliminary design in black and white, then towards dawn mix his colours and, as the light grew, apply them to the under-painting. With this erratic timetable it was quite usual for his team to be on duty for 18 hours at a stretch, with few breaks for sleep in between. Sometimes Jack and Clifford met for breakfast at 2.00 a.m. in order to begin plastering at 3.00; they then took time off for a nap between 10.00 and 11.00, returning at midday when Rivera arrived to start painting, both of them often remaining on site till 8.00 or 9.00 in the evening. It was a tough regime. 'It is simply awful having to get out of a warm bed at eleven or twelve to go to work,'[121] Clifford complained. 'And the trouble is that I never want to sleep during the daytime.'

Despite the enormous pressure he was under, Diego usually appeared relaxed, sometimes strolling in mid-morning to stand chatting with a group of Mexican friends, or sitting reading the comic strips in the papers while smoking a big Garcia Grande cigar. Once he began work, however, he became so completely absorbed that time ceased to exist. As Frida put it, '[Diego] does not live a life that could be called normal. His amount of energy breaks all clocks and calendars.'[122] Throughout the day people came in to watch him at work, often staff from the Institute or from the Ford office, standing silently looking up at the scaffold. The great room was usually quiet, the assistants absorbed in their various duties, on a platform above them the portly figure of Rivera in workman's overalls, in one hand a white enamel plate on which were his colours, in the other his brushes. Nothing seemed to distract him, yet he was always ready to talk, while never breaking off what he was doing. Later he wrote of his time in Detroit, 'During that year I did as much as I could and lived what was perhaps the best and most fruitful period of my life.'[123]

---

[121] Clifford Wight to JH 14.12.32. HRC.
[122] *The Letters of Frida Kahlo.* p. 150.
[123] *Portrait of America*, Diego Rivera (Allen & Unwin, 1935) p. 18.

Rivera was so appreciative and inspirational that none of his staff grudged the long hours: as Ernst Halberstadt put it, 'I admired the hard work he put in himself, and nobody would have worked as hard as we did if he hadn't set the example.'[124] Yet while apparently easy-going, Rivera had no hesitation in making his feelings clear if any of his assistants fell short. Jack was scolded more than once for working too slowly; and on another occasion, Diego lost his temper when he was told that the panel on which he had been working for 23 hours would have to be completely redone because Jack had made a mistake with the dimensions. 'What *is* the use of continuing this work?' he shouted, throwing down his palette. But then he quickly pulled himself together, patted a very contrite Jack on the shoulder, and immediately prepared to begin again.

As before in San Francisco, Cristina was left to occupy herself during the long hours when her husband was at work. And as before she found a supportive friend in Frida. As they both lived in the same building it was easy for them to spend time together, talking, cooking, shopping and exploring the city. Both were shocked by some of the sights they saw, the long lines of unemployed, in the shops the piles of tinned dog food, the main source of nourishment for many homeless families. At midday Frida, usually accompanied by Cristina, went over to the Garden Court, bringing lunch in a big covered basket for Diego and his team.

The two women had found a Mexican grocery store, to Frida's delight as she disdained most American food. Diego would come down from the scaffold, usually joined by Jack, Clifford and one or two of their colleagues whom Frida always encouraged to join them, all of them sitting on upturned wooden crates to eat. After lunch Frida usually stayed, drawing, knitting, reading, or simply watching her husband at work, while Cristina went off on her own. She spent many afternoons in the local library choosing books on art for Jack to read, hoping this would help him towards a more

---

[124] *The Mexican Muralists in the United States.* p. 138.

successful career. Elegant as ever, she also made frequent visits to her dressmaker, a local woman whose main business came from sewing clothes for what she referred to as 'sporting girls', in other words the prostitutes of the neighbourhood.

With Frida spending so many hours at the Institute, Cristina was glad of the company of the newest member of the group, Lucienne Bloch. Lucienne, a clever, vivacious girl with dark hair and a round face, was delighted to be reunited with the Riveras and for the opportunity of working for Diego. Shortly after arriving in Detroit she had dropped in on Clifford's wife, Jean, also living at the Wardell. Cristina had been with her, and Lucienne, rather thrown by Cristina's dignified manner, immediately launched into her repertoire of funny faces, with which she often had success at parties. '[I] acted crazy,'[125] she recalled, 'and showed all my parlor tricks – rose petal on lips, lion face, Chinese face … and played my lute which I had brought over at last moment, thank God.' Fortunately Cristina appeared unfazed by such frenzied showing-off and a couple of days later invited Lucienne with the Riveras to dinner at the apartment. Here for the first time Lucienne met Jack, who conducted himself in his customary, rather self-effacing manner. 'A rather weak English type but nice,'[126] she noted in her diary. When dinner was over Lucienne again played her lute while Frida sang, after which Diego retired to bed and Jack took the three women to a speakeasy for cocktails.

Lucienne's duties at the Garden Court were not particularly onerous, and she had rather more free time than the others. This suited Cristina, delighted to have a congenial companion with whom to go on expeditions. 'I did a lot of gallivanting with Cristina Hastings,'[127] wrote Lucienne, who became genuinely fond of her 'fantastic' new friend, despite finding her manner occasionally disconcerting, particularly 'the way she rolls her eyes

---

[125] Lucienne Bloch diaries.
[126] Ibid.
[127] Lucienne Bloch to Linda Bank Downs 17.4.78. Copy Detroit Institute of Arts.

– almost too much and by the enthusiasm for all odds and ends'.[128] During the long, hot days of summer the two women visited the zoo, played tennis, watched baseball, went swimming, picnicked in the park and on the banks of Lake Erie; they drove through the poorest parts of the city as well as the prosperous residential districts; they spent a day at Belle Isle where they watched the sailing boats on Lake St Clair and ate quantities of hot dogs and Eskimo pies. 'Cristina is always hungry',[129] Lucienne noted. One of the most memorable of their outings was a visit to the Ford plant at Dearborn, where they were both fascinated and appalled by the pressure of the work, by the heat and noise; fascinated, too, while eating lunch in the canteen to catch sight of Prince Louis Ferdinand, loaded tray in hand, wandering around looking for somewhere to sit. 'A fine head',[130] Lucienne noted, 'among the other American brutes all pale and sick.'

Frida sometimes joined them on these expeditions, as did Jean Wight. In Jack's photograph album is a picture of Jean, Frida and Cristina, all three looking rather solemn, Frida in the middle, a fragile figure, bareheaded in an ankle-length dress and long shawl, Jean and Cristina in hats, high heels and fur-collared coats. Frida kept a copy of the same photograph, but in her version the picture is mutilated, the head and torso of the central figure excised.

Despite the sombre mood caused by the Depression, as soon as the Riveras arrived in Detroit they were much sought after for dinners, dances and teas, with the Hastingses and Wights usually included in the invitations. 'The aristocratic Lord Hastings' was generally considered a delightful young man, his unfailingly courteous manner an asset at any gathering; his wife, however, was viewed more warily, described as 'sophisticated but manic-depressive',[131] 'an absolutely nutty Italian, who cared for nothing'.

---

[128] Lucienne Bloch diaries.
[129] Ibid.
[130] Ibid.
[131] Edgar Preston Richardson interview with Linda Bank Downs 6.2.78. Detroit Institute of Arts.

Most congenial of their hosts were Edsel and Eleanor Ford, who lived in a vast Cotswold-style mansion at Grosse Pointe. Diego liked and respected Edsel, despite his wealth and his capitalist views, the two men forming a genuine friendship, bolstered by Edsel's generosity and charm, his love of art and admiration for Diego's painting in particular. They were also entertained by Robert Tannahill, millionaire nephew of Eleanor Ford and himself an important collector; and by Albert Kahn, the architect of the Rouge plant, who had donated some notable works of art to the city. These were part of a cultured, sophisticated section of society, all wealthy but whose moderate politics were at some considerable distance from the rigid far right of Edsel's father.

At Henry Ford's Fair Lane estate in Dearborn the atmosphere was very different. Henry Ford, tall, silver-haired, immaculately turned out, received his guests with a courteous formality. At Fair Lane the evenings were much more structured and conventional, the company rather older and invariably conservative. There was a certain amount of whispered disdain, particularly among the Grosse Pointe matrons, for Frida's Mexican costumes, impatience with Diego's ungrammatical English, and in general a slightly condescending manner towards these funny-looking foreigners, this eccentric troupe of bohemian artists.

Frida, who preferred to refuse such invitations and accompanied Diego only under protest, was more than once provoked to retaliate: pretending innocence she talked communism to Henry Ford's sister, mocked the Pope in a Catholic household, and sweetly enquired of Henry Ford himself, a proud and vigorous anti-Semite, if he were Jewish. She loathed 'those fucking parties',[132] she told her friend and confidant, Dr Eloesser, those people, 'with their hypocrisy and disgusting Puritanism, their Protestant sermons, their limitless pretentiousness'.

After the first two or three weeks, however, the pace of their social life inevitably slowed. After a long day at the Institute

---

[132] *The Letters of Frida Kahlo.* p. 108.

Diego, Jack and Clifford were usually too tired to go out, and when they returned to the Wardell often preferred to spend the evening together. Jack particularly enjoyed the occasions when Frida cooked dinner for everyone, the women chatting to her in the kitchen, the three men sitting smoking and talking in the next room. Frida, concerned about Diego's weight, had recently put her husband on a strict diet of mainly citrus fruit and vegetable juice, to which with extraordinary fortitude he was resolutely adhering, seemingly unconcerned while the others ate Frida's delicious duck *mole* or *arroz con pollo*.

In these gatherings the odd one out, as always, was Clifford's wife: Jean was dull, humourless and easily shocked. She was also indiscreet, repeating to Cliff private conversations which inevitably landed one of the others in trouble. A typical incident came after Jack described to Frida a fall he had had on the scaffold, at which Lucienne argued that Edsel Ford should pay to make the structure safer. 'And what did Jean do but tell Cliff all this but all mixed up',[133] with the result that Clifford was furious with Lucienne, told her it was none of her business, and if she were going to tell tales like that she should stay away from the Institute.

It was soon after this contretemps that Lucienne suddenly announced she wanted to return for a few days to New York to see a boyfriend: would Cristina like to go with her? The two were in the car at the time, and 'Cristina not only consented but was so excited she passed 3 red stop signals in the traffic.'[134] Leaving Detroit in the last week of June, they drove through Ohio, Pennsylvania, New Jersey, until finally at eight o'clock in the evening they arrived at Newark from where they could see the distant skyscrapers glowing in the sunset, and, Lucienne recalled, 'Cristina and I just yelled "Oh boy Oh boy Oh boy!!"'[135] The two of them immensely enjoyed their short holiday, and years later Lucienne wrote to Jack that she always looked back with pleasure

---

[133] Lucienne Bloch diaries.
[134] Ibid.
[135] Ibid.

on the 'trip with Cristina, the rain storm over Lake Erie, the sun burn, the AAA Tourist house at Indiana, PA. Why are these memories so vivid to me?'[136]

Shortly after they returned a crisis erupted with Frida. For some while Frida had been feeling unwell: her back hurt, she was permanently tired, and in May, less than a month after arriving in Detroit, she discovered she was two months pregnant. Immediately she wrote to Dr Eloesser for counsel. She knew Diego did not want a child, and she herself was worried that, much as she longed for it, she was not strong enough to carry it to term: should she have an abortion? she asked him. 'I do not have enough confidence in Jean Wight and Cristina Hastings to consult with them about things like this which have an enormous importance and which because of one false move can take me to the grave!'[137] But then early on the morning of 4 July Frida started to haemorrhage and had to be rushed to hospital by ambulance, a distraught Diego following by taxi. He returned a few hours later in a state of great anxiety; for once he was too worried to work, frantic for news of Frida's condition. In the hope of distracting him, Jack took him off to Cadillac Square to watch the Fourth of July parade, but Diego was too restless and unhappy, and they had to give up and return to the hospital. It was nearly three weeks before Frida, deeply depressed by her failed pregnancy, was finally discharged and came home.

At the end of the following month the Hastingses left Detroit for Chicago. Jack's commission to execute a mural for the forthcoming World's Fair was his first opportunity to work for an employer who was neither patron nor friend. When the offer arrived, Diego, who believed in his assistant's talent, had been extremely encouraging, wholly supporting this move to further his career. '[Rivera] insisted on my leaving,'[138] Jack said later, 'because I'd had some quite good propositions elsewhere.' Jack was enthused by the prospect of what

---

[136] Lucienne Bloch to JH 21.9.37. HRC.
[137] *Frida: a Biography of Frida Kahlo.* p. 139.
[138] JH interview with Loyd Grossman. *Telegraph* Magazine, 1981.

lay ahead, although it was a wrench to leave the close-knit circle in Detroit. After working so long and so intensely together, the leave-taking was inevitably emotional. Fortunately the prospect of reunion was in the near future, as Rivera had himself won an important commission for the Fair. Meanwhile Jack and Clifford promised to keep regularly in touch by letter.

On one of the hottest days of the summer, the Hastingses set out for the day's drive to Chicago. Before starting work on the mural for the Fair, Jack had agreed to undertake several unpaid projects for friends. The first was for James Glaser, an exact contemporary whom Jack had first met in London in the 1920s. Jim Glaser, now a well-to-do grain-broker living with his family in the affluent Chicago suburb of Glencoe, had been delighted to renew contact, and had asked Jack to paint a fresco in his basement bar, officially referred to at this period as the 'refreshment room'. The subject decided on, appropriately, was The History of Bootlegging.

Chicago in the early 1930s was widely regarded as the crime capital of the United States, one of the most dangerous and lawless cities in the world. Since the passing of the 18th Amendment in January 1920, prohibiting the sale, production and importing of alcohol, Chicago had been taken over by rival gangs fighting to control the immensely lucrative business of smuggling and selling illegal liquor. Competition between the gangs was fierce, with up to 200 robberies and murders reported every night, and during this period the most famous, feared and powerful of the mobsters was the notorious Al Capone. For years Capone had run the city as his personal fiefdom, amassing a private fortune of over $42 million, and avoiding arrest by the simple expedient of paying generous bribes to Chicago's law-enforcement officers. But finally in October 1931 Capone was brought to trial and convicted not of bootlegging or murder but of tax evasion, for which he received a sentence of 11 years. Needless to say the trial was widely covered, with journalists arriving from all over the world (among them Margaret Lane, 'special correspondent' for the Daily Express and eventually to be Jack Hastings's second wife).

Capone proved an irresistible subject, and Jack was diligent in his research, talking to police as well as gang members, visiting jails and attending identity parades. 'The detective bureau's nightly "show-up" of prisoners was greeted last night by the presence of Lord and Lady Hastings of London,'[139] one local paper reported. 'The couple came in character of observers, however, rather than participants.' Jack also explored the local speakeasies, usually concealed in the back rooms of shops or in the basements of apartment buildings, where drink was served in china tea-cups, the often vile taste of cheaply manufactured gin and whisky disguised by the new cocktail mixes suddenly in fashion.

The painting in Jim Glaser's bar, extending across the width of one wall, had at its centre the seated and instantly recognisable figure of Capone, in spats and white fedora, cigar in hand, flanked on either side by his henchmen and with a platinum-blond floozie lolling on his knee; behind him is a banner on which is inscribed 'CONSTITUTION OF THE UNITED STATES XVIIITH AMENDMENT', and to right and left are shown the various processes of the bootlegging business: the smuggling in of contraband supplies by water, road and air, the manufacture in illegal stills, the ferocious gun-battles between gangs as well as with federal agents attempting to stop the trade.

Once completed, the work attracted some attention in the society columns in the city's press. One shows a picture of the fresco, the bespectacled artist standing before it, brush and palette in hand, while his wife, glamorously dressed in a pretty summer dress and high heels, stands beside him flashing a glittering smile at the photographer. The only adverse criticism came from one of Capone's old cronies who objected to the portrayal of the gangster's moll. 'Al never gave a tumble to a skirt like that,'[140] he said disgustedly. 'He wouldn't give her a job washin' glasses in a speak ...' Of rather greater interest to Jack was the reaction from

---

[139] *Berkeley Daily Gazette*, 7.1.33.
[140] *Chicago Herald*, 1935.

Detroit. 'I must write and congratulate you on your fine work',[141] Clifford wrote after seeing photographs of the mural. 'I think it's swell! ... You ought to get a commission from Capone when he gets out! ... Diego was very enthusiastic about it. He thinks you have made great strides ... When are you coming to Detroit? We do really miss you ever so much ... We are so eager to see you again,'[142] Clifford continued, 'and while we haven't a "refreshment room" in the basement, we have a few gallons of home-brew wine if Chicago hasn't spoiled you for such tame fare.'

The friend whom Jack was most eager to see was his old Oxford companion, the explorer, William McGovern. McGovern, married and with three children, was now an Associate Professor of Political Science at Northwestern University. As handsome and charming as ever, McGovern was delighted to be reunited with the Hastingses, 'both crazy people but quite amusing',[143] as he affectionately described them. In McGovern's house in Evanston, the two men reminisced for hours about the past, about McGovern's expedition to the Amazon and Peru, Jack's life in Australia and the South Pacific. While they talked, Jack worked on a portrait of the glamorous adventurer sitting at a desk in suit and tie, a faraway expression in his eyes, a map of the world behind him. When Lucienne Bloch came over from Detroit to see the Hastingses, Jack introduced her to McGovern, whom she found disturbingly attractive. 'He is typical English',[144] she noted. 'He loathes nature, prefers 42nd St to all places in the world, makes exotic cocktails and doesn't show at first glance what a fantastic lot of knowledge he has about everything under the sun. I was dying to find fault with his wife and to really fall for him but outside of genuine admiration I couldn't make myself be so catty.'

One snowy winter evening Cristina took Lucienne to hear McGovern lecture, after which the two women with the McGoverns

---

141 Clifford Wight to JH 20.9.32. HRC.
142 Clifford Wight to JH 23.11.32. HRC.
143 William McGovern to Mary Donahey 1.3.38. Northwestern University.
144 Lucienne Bloch diaries.

went back to the Hastingses apartment, where Jack had promised to have dinner ready. Almost immediately the visitors found themselves witnessing one of the rare occasions when Jack lost control of his temper. As they walked through the door they smelt burning. 'Cristina nearly screamed when she saw Jack had let the pot roast burn,'[145] wrote Lucienne. 'She cried and made a hysterical scene and I saw miracle of miracles, Jack getting excited so that she cooled down quickly – for if he gets excited it must mean that he's on the point of breaking a blood vessel.' As Lucienne was quick to notice, the moment Jack showed anger Cristina grew calm: she had got what she wanted, a reaction from her opponent. Once the explosion over the ruined pot-roast had died down, Cristina went cheerfully out to buy some cold ham, after which everyone did their best to enjoy the rest of the evening.

During their stay in Chicago both Hastingses were deluged with invitations, for which Jack had little time, although Cristina was pleased to meet new people and have something to do. The gossip columns faithfully reported Lady Hastings's presence at luncheons and dinners, her taking part in a table-setting contest, attending a tea in honour of Vita Sackville-West, and giving a talk at a fashionable boutique on her life in the South Seas. Her constant companions, a pet chameleon and a white kitten called Mimi, had their own share of attention, while Cristina's exotic looks and flair for fashion received much admiring comment: on one occasion she appeared dashingly dressed in a brown corduroy skirt, silver-studded cowboy belt, beige sweater and necklace of shark's teeth; at a private view she was memorably compared, with her 'dark hair, prominent eyes and many white teeth through open lips,'[146] to 'a medieval saint in perpetual ecstasy'.

Yet beneath the glamorous veneer, Cristina was not happy. Still in love with her husband, she was frustrated beyond bearing by his apparent indifference to her frequent rages; she, who recovered

---

[145] Ibid.
[146] *Chicago Tribune*, 30.10.32.

within minutes from even the most violent outbursts, never understood the scarring and wretchedness these scenes caused his peaceable nature; nor did she ever quite fathom the depth of feeling that lay beneath that courteous manner, the emotions that from childhood he had learned to protect and conceal.

Jack meanwhile was deeply absorbed in his work. He had painted several portraits, as well as a mural, long since disappeared, for Northwestern University; and he also had a small one-man show at the Increase Robinson Gallery, which included half a dozen paintings from the South Seas. 'The most elusive man in Chicago is Lord Hastings', began one article. 'Luncheons, tea, cocktails, dinner or dancing have simply been out as far as he is concerned for several weeks and will be until the World's Fair opens.'

The author of this piece was Mrs Henry Field, whom Jack had met three years earlier in Jamaica. Then Betty Sturges had been a ravishing and lively young woman with whom, while staying with her family, he had enjoyed a brief affair. Now married to the first of her five husbands, a distinguished anthropologist with a big house on Lake Shore Drive, Betty was a busy hostess, social editor for the Chicago *Herald*, and as pretty and flirtatious as ever. Jack was of course delighted to see her: less so Cristina, instantly alert to the danger. In Cristina's scrapbook there is a cut-out picture of a corpulent nude over whose head is pasted a photograph of Betty; and at about this time, Cristina suddenly left Chicago, disappearing for a couple of weeks to California.

But for Jack his main concern was his mural for the World's Fair. The theme of the Fair, due to open in June 1933, was 'A Century of Progress', the project intended largely to provide a desperately needed boost to the dire state of the Illinois economy. Although for financial reasons the original plans had been considerably scaled down, the design for the site was none the less impressive, with especially commissioned buildings stretching over 400 acres along the banks of Lake Michigan. The most prominent of these was the Hall of Science, one section of which was dedicated to medicine; here in a small lecture-theatre was a display of dentistry, and this was the area that Jack, for a fee of 700 dollars, was to decorate. On the two walls at his disposal, he painted three panels, the first showing a dentist at work against a background of a busy cityscape; the second, a farming family growing the crops necessary for strong teeth; and the third, again a dentist with his patient, but here surrounded by a community of Mexican peasants.

The panels were of aluminium, each so large that the artist had some difficulty in finding a studio big enough to house them. Eventually he ended up in the City Mortuary, in many ways an ideal venue as while in the morgue he could work almost entirely undisturbed. 'It was very quiet,'[147] Jack recalled in an interview, 'with only the occasional corpse being brought in.' Because the panels had to be completely finished before they were installed there was no time for the traditional fresco technique: instead Jack speedily coated the panels by means of a spray-gun, a method pioneered by one of Rivera's compatriots, David Siqueiros. When the Fair opened to a great fanfare on 27 May, Jack was thrilled and astonished to see on the first day a long line waiting to enter the Dental Exhibition: when he finally made his way to the head of the queue he found the attraction to be not his murals but a set of George Washington's false teeth.

It was while Jack was in the early stages of planning his dentistry mural that Clifford, accompanied by Jean, arrived in Chicago: he had come not only to try and find work for himself but to prepare the way for Diego's own project, a fresco for the General Motors building at the Fair. The two couples were delighted to see each other, with the Hastingses eager for news from Detroit. They had been much missed by the Riveras, Clifford told them. 'They think an awful lot of you & Jack ... & I think Diego would love to have Jack helping him again.'[148] Meanwhile Clifford had much to relate. Frida's mother had died, and Frida had left for Mexico City

[147] JH interview with Loyd Grossman. *Telegraph* Magazine, 1981.
[148] Clifford Wight to Cristina Hastings 12.12.32. HRC.

where she stayed for over two months; Diego at the Institute had continued working at a furious rate while still keeping resolutely to his diet, on which he eventually lost over 100 pounds: when on Frida's return Diego went to meet her at the station, wearing a suit of Clifford's as his own no longer fitted, Frida barely recognised him. Now Frida wrote to Clifford asking him about Chicago – 'Do you think I will like it?'[149] – and sending her love to her friends. 'Give many kisses to Jean and Cristina (with the permission of Jack) and un abrazo a usted y a Jack without permission at all ... Diego send his best wishes to all of you.'

The topic that dominated everything, however, was the uproar that had greeted the unveiling of the Garden Court murals, which Diego had finally finished in the second week of March 1933. Immediately the churches and large sections of society furiously condemned them as vulgar, blasphemous and un-American, with the chief objection, inevitably, focused on the scene depicting the vaccination of the child and its suspicious resemblance to the Nativity ('but all children wear haloes,'[150] said Rivera disingenuously). There were angry demands that the frescoes be destroyed, or at least removed; according to a front-page editorial in The *Detroit News*, 'The best thing to do would be to whitewash the entire work and completely return the court to its original beauty.'[151]

Fortunately Edsel Ford was having none of it, fiercely defending the artist and his work. With the issue angrily debated in the papers and on the radio, crowds such as the Institute had never seen before came pouring in to the Garden Court. Jack, who had been appalled by the reaction to Rivera's masterpiece, was gratified to hear of this unforeseen result. 'From the one or two hundred people who visit the Museum on Saturdays and Sundays

[149] Frida Kahlo to Clifford Wight 11.4.33. Detroit Institute of Arts.
[150] *Dreaming with his Eyes Open: a Life of Diego Rivera*, Patrick Marnham (Bloomsbury, 1998) p. 262.
[151] *Detroit News*, 18.3.33.

the attendance rose to over fifteen thousand a day,'[152] he wrote in an article, '[and] the police had to begin to move out the crowd at four o'clock to clear the building by six.' Within days a long comic verse satirising the situation was going the rounds:

> ... At last the job was finished and
> The people flocked inside,
> The clergy took one hasty look
> And they were horrified!
> They pointed shaking fingers at
> The panel of diseases,
> And said the vaccinated child
> Was no one else but Jesus! ...
>
> Oh, jolly old Diego,
> His enemies abound-o ...
>
> That fresco-paintin', aggravatin'
> Son-of-a-gun Diego!
>
> About the meaning of the work
> There grew an awful schism,
> Some people called the frescoes art
> Some called 'em communism.
> They said: 'If you had shown our soul
> We wouldn't so much mind it.'
> Rivera said: 'I looked for it,
> But gosh, I couldn't find it.'
> ...[153]

And so on.

But the scandal in Detroit was as nothing to the furore that shortly afterwards erupted in New York. Before going on to Chicago, Rivera had been contracted to paint a mural in Rockefeller

---

[152] JH unpublished article, HRC.
[153] Franklin M. Peck. Detroit Institute of Arts.

Center, the theme an overview of contemporary and scientific culture to be entitled *Man at the Crossroads*. It was only when the fresco was almost completed that it was noticed a portrait of Lenin had quietly materialised by the side of the main figure – a portrait which had very definitely not been part of the original design. Immediately furious objections were expressed at this disgraceful instance of 'red propaganda'; Rivera was sacked, the mural covered up and shortly afterwards destroyed. When the news reached Chicago, General Motors instantly cancelled his World's Fair contract. Although in public Rivera dealt bravely with the scandal, in fact he was deeply wounded by it and depressed by the obliteration of his work.

Jack for his part was appalled at Diego's treatment, and the sequence of events in New York served to strengthen his already staunch anti-capitalism. Two years later he was to pay tribute to Diego and the desecrated fresco in a communist-themed mural painted for the Karl Marx Memorial Library in London.

With the dentistry mural finished, Jack had little reason to remain in Chicago; more to the point, his visa, and Cristina's, were about to expire. Their permits had already been renewed once, with some difficulty, through the personal intervention of Edsel Ford; but now they both felt it was time to leave the States. Towards the end of July 1933 they drove to New York to see the Riveras, who were planning to remain a while longer as Diego still had work in hand. With typical generosity Diego suggested the Hastingses should stay at his house in Mexico City until he and Frida returned there. Elated by the prospect, Jack and Cristina left New York at the beginning of August, sailing via Havana, and docking at Vera Cruz, before making their way inland to the capital.

From the moment he arrived Jack was captivated by Mexico, 'one of the most beautiful countries I have ever seen,'[154] he said later. He and Cristina were both enchanted by the Riveras' house at San Angel: designed by the architect Juan O'Gorman, it is

---

[154] JH to James Norman Hall 4.1.36. HRC.

a strikingly modernist structure, two separate cubic dwellings linked by a bridge on the top storey, Diego's, much the larger, painted pink, Frida's blue house smaller and more compact. Both had spacious studios, and Jack felt immediately at home in Diego's large work-room, an attractive muddle of papier-mâché figures, pottery, masks, skeletons, piles of paper, bookcases crammed with books and periodicals, easels, opened cartons, and stacks of half-finished canvases.

During the nine months they spent in the country, Jack painted landscapes and portraits, baroque churches, white-washed villages, Mayan pyramids and Aztec ruins, as well as many aspects of Mexico City itself, often with the sinister outline of the volcano, Popocatépetl, lowering over the horizon.

When at the end of the year the Riveras arrived from the States, Jack and Cristina moved out to a small house next door. The débâcle in New York had left Diego cast down, and largely as a result of his stringent diet he felt apathetic and unwell. He was visibly cheered to be reunited with the Hastingses, however, and much enjoyed being driven about in their car, acting as guide on expeditions through the surrounding country, as well as further afield to Tehuantepec and Chichén Itzá. They had all hoped that Clifford might join them: 'if you go to MEXICO',[155] Frida had told him, 'you will meet there the loveliest people on earth, the Riveras and the Hastings. What do you think of that? ... we'll be ... oh boy all together !!!!!! happy !!!!!! ...' But Clifford was working in San Francisco and unable to leave.

While together in Chicago the Wights and Hastingses had attended a series of lectures on Marxism, which they had found inspirational; and now evening after evening in the company of the Riveras the subject was exhaustively explored. For the rest of his life Jack held the greatest respect for Diego's thinking, influenced not only by his particular form of communism but by the humanity and lack of prejudice in his political philosophy,

---

[155] Frida Kahlo to Clifford Wight 29.10.33. Detroit Institute of Arts.

and impressed, too, by his insatiable curiosity. An admirer of Montaigne, Diego often approvingly quoted the axiom, 'where doubt ends, stupidity begins'. In all this he was passionately supported by his wife. 'I am more and more convinced',[156] Frida stated, 'that the only way to become a man, I mean a human being and not an animal, is to be a communist.'

During their lengthy conversations, painting was of course discussed at length, and when Jack tentatively suggested that Diego might like to hold an exhibition in London, he was gratified by the enthusiastic response.

Rivera was keen to visit England again – he had been there only once as a very young man – and seized eagerly on Jack's suggestion of a show at the Tate. On his return to London, Jack had little difficulty in selling the idea to the Gallery, but unfortunately his letter to Diego, enclosing the official offer, was mislaid in the muddle of the studio in San Angel; and there it lay buried for over a year – by which time the proposed date for the exhibition had passed. When he eventually unearthed the correspondence, Diego was contrite and sent an apologetic letter to Jack: 'Dear Jack, I dare to answer your letter of a year ago solely because I believe that it is a record in delayed answers ...'[157] To this Frida attached a little note of her own: 'Dear Jack and Cristi ... If it is arranged that Diego goes to London I will see you and tell you many things I can't in this letter. Please write me and tell me how are you both ... All my love to you Frida.' ...

The Hastingses remained in Mexico until the spring of 1934 when, after four and a half years away, they decided to return home. The parting from the Riveras was painful, although at this stage they all believed they would meet again in London. Meanwhile Diego's influence proved invaluable at the point of departure: the day before their ship was due to sail, Jack's paintings were seized by Customs, on the assumption that he was attempting to export

---

[156] Frida Kahlo to Clifford Wight 29.10.33. Ibid.
[157] Diego Rivera to JH 25.4.36. HRC.

Mexican works of art. Luckily Diego was able to intercede – 'Sr Hastings[158] … es un artista muy interesante y un excelente amigo mio …'[159] – and the couple embarked without further incident. Looking back some years later Jack wrote in an article how he still missed 'the comradeship of my Mexican friends, and above all the friendship and constant inspiration of Diego Rivera'.

---

[158] Diego Rivera to Marte R. Gomez 18..4.34. HRC.
[159] ('Sr Hastings is a very interesting artist and an excellent friend of mine') …

9

Towards a haven of peace and rest

After an unbroken absence of almost five years, the Hastingses returned to England in the early summer of 1934. According to Alec Waugh, who was delighted to see his old friends again, they were both in high spirits. Whether this can have been entirely true is open to doubt: parting from the Riveras had been hard, and for Jack in particular it was a wrench leaving the Americas, although he could hardly have known he would never see Diego nor set foot on the continent again.

Now he and Cristina were faced with setting up a permanent home together, despite the fact that the marriage was under strain. The last few years had been a constant adventure, enabling them for long periods largely to ignore the unsatisfactory aspects of their relationship, but could they now settle down and spend the rest of their lives peaceably together? Jack knew they could not, and once more begged Cristina to divorce him; yet again she refused, and as she had given him no grounds to divorce her, there was – for the present – nothing further to be done.

Their most immediate concern was to find somewhere to live, and here a friend of Cristina's from her early days in London provided a solution. Alice Astor, beautiful and immensely rich, had known both Hastingses before they were married, although it was Cristina to whom she was closer. With her first husband, Alice had moved into a magnificent Regency villa, Hanover Lodge, in Regent's Park, where she was now ensconced with her second husband, Raimund von Hofmannstahl. The house, which stood on the Outer Circle, overlooking the canal and with four acres of garden, was approached through iron gates on either side of

which were two small gatehouses. It was these that Alice offered
to the Hastingses as temporary accommodation, her generosity
acknowledged by Jack with a painting in water-colour of Hanover
Lodge. Although somewhat confined, the two little houses suited
their way of life very well, one for themselves, the other for their
six-year-old daughter Moorea.

During her parents' absence abroad, Moorea had been living
at Burton with her grandparents. Maud had dispatched regular
bulletins to Jack about the child's progress, and indeed the
moulding of Moorea was now her chief occupation; although she
accepted that the child, once her parents returned, must of course
live with them, she had very clear plans for her future. Oddly,
although Maud was undoubtedly devoted, meticulously organising every detail of her granddaughter's day, she herself spent
little time with her. Moorea had her own quarters in the nursery
wing, where she spent most of her time when not in the garden or
out riding with one of the grooms; following family tradition, she
was first introduced to the hunt at the age of six.

Every afternoon Moorea was brought down by her nurse on
the dot of 5.00 p.m. to spend the traditional hour with her grandparents in the drawing-room. During this hour Maud took almost
no notice, preferring to sit reading the paper in front of the fire,
and it was her grandfather, Warner, who played with the little
girl, going down on all fours and hiding behind the sofa for their
favourite game of bears. According to Jack's sister Norah, who had
always included Moorea in holidays with her own daughters in
Ireland, she was the centre of his life. 'I cannot attempt to describe
in words Dada's devotion to that child,' Norah told Jack. 'He simply
adores her, and plays with her by the hour. Both parents quite
realise that you and Cristina will naturally want Moorea, and are
quite resigned etc about losing her, but, Dada especially, will miss
her dreadfully.'

Predictably, the war over Moorea's education quickly escalated
between Maud and the Hastingses. Maud wanted her given a
conventional Anglican upbringing, lessons with a governess at

home, with tutors for music, dancing and deportment, all to prepare her for her first season as a débutante and the eventual landing of a suitable husband. 'Would Lavinia (Duchess of Norfolk) have made the marriage she has done if she had *not* been properly *brought up* & received all the advantages a child can get in a comfortable country house?' Maud argued forcefully. 'Look at little Princess Elizabeth, *always* with her parents, & seeing the right kind of people every day. I hear she is *wonderful*.'

But Jack and Cristina had other ideas: Moorea was to be sent away to boarding-school, and even more shocking, to Dartington Hall in Devon, a newly founded, extremely experimental establishment with no compulsory lessons, no punishment, no uniforms, and whose pupils were allowed to do very much as they pleased.

All this was anathema to Maud, who was especially outraged by the total absence of religious instruction.

What are you doing for your little girl, shunting her off to a queer rough school to be brought up by an atheist where she has no *chance* of filling the *position* she should take up one day ... For many generations we have been Christian people Jack & it seems to us the *greatest wrong* you can do a little child is to bring her up as an *atheist* ... What more *wonderful* teaching can you give a little child than the teaching of Jesus, & the lovely Xmas story.

For Moorea this must have been a confusing period, although looking back she claimed not have been particularly unhappy while growing up. At Burton she enjoyed the life outdoors, the kind servants, the large garden, the horses and dogs, and she quickly became devoted to her grandfather, although Maud remained a remote, rather alarming figure. Her parents she saw rarely: holidays were spent at Burton and with her Aunt Norah at Mourne, and she was in London for only a week or two at a time.

After a few months the Hastingses moved from their double-dwelling in Regent's Park and into a house in St John's Wood, but even then there was little family life. Moorea at this period remembered her father as a benign but distant figure, while of

Cristina she remained extremely wary. 'My mother occasionally took me out,' she recalled. 'We sometimes went for walks in the park, or to the Zoo, and once she took me to Madame Tussaud's. But mostly I was too frightened to enjoy it. Her rages seemed to come out of nowhere and they absolutely terrified me.'

By the beginning of 1935, the Hastingses had left Hanover Lodge for a pleasant house, 45 Wellington Road, next to St John's Wood Underground Station. ('Which is the most easily remembered telephone number?' asked the *Daily Telegraph* soon after the move. 'That of Viscount Hastings: Primrose 1066.') Here the rent was conveniently low because the air-vent for the station was in the middle of the garden and the rumbling of the trains could be heard far into the night. Jack painted a fresco on the staircase – two men drilling in a rocky landscape for the minerals from which paints are made – and Cristina with her usual flair arranged the furniture which had so long been left in store.

The house was just large enough for husband and wife to have separate quarters, for Jack had made it clear that although in public he and Cristina would continue to appear as man and wife, from now on his private life was to be largely his own concern. Inevitably Cristina showed her distress at the growing distance between them through ever more frequent scenes, and while Jack found her explosive temper increasingly hard to bear, she was made equally miserable by his impenetrable detachment.

For the Hastingses the one important bond that remained was political. With the situation in Europe alarmingly unstable, on their return from abroad they were anxious to find out all they could. 'They wanted to know what people in England were feeling about it all',[160] wrote Alec Waugh. 'Cristina's eyes would blaze as she discussed the situation.' During their time in the States, both Hastingses had been profoundly influenced by Rivera, and also by what they had seen for themselves of the harrowing consequences of the Great Depression.

---

[160] *The Best Wine Last*. p. 54.

For Jack a moment of enlightenment had come during his painting of the Al Capone mural. 'I really swung over to socialism',[161] he said in an interview, 'when I worked on a mural for a wheat-broker in Chicago and wheat was being burnt outside the city while half the population starved.' While in the States he had read and been greatly impressed by Spengler's *The Decline of the West*, and more recently by *The Coming Struggle for Power* by John Strachey, an Eton and Oxford contemporary of Jack's, in which the origins and development of capitalism are examined from a Marxist viewpoint.

Like many of his generation, he had been imprinted with Lincoln Steffens's famous declaration about Russia – 'I have seen the future and it works!'; and increasingly he was attracted by the promise held out by the Soviet Union, struck by John Strachey's statement, "To travel from the capitalist world into Soviet territory is to pass from death to birth."[162]

Curious to see for himself the reality of this brave new world, in 1935 Jack with Alec Waugh planned a three-week trip to Moscow. 'I wanted to see what the Russian Revolution had given birth to in the way of art,'[163] he explained, 'and what impressions the Soviet would have on my own mind.' With every step of their programme rigidly prescribed by Stalin's Intourist agency, they knew they would have little freedom to explore, yet it was none the less an intriguing prospect. They left from Liverpool Street Station at the beginning of February, going first to the Netherlands ('Jack slept right through Holland',[164] Alec recorded), then to Berlin and Warsaw, before finally arriving in Russia.

The four days and nights on the train seemed to go on for ever, the two of them cooped up in an overheated compartment, both with bad colds, bickering and fidgeting and generally getting on each other's nerves. On 9 February they finally arrived in

---

[161] *The Guardian*, 20.6.69.
[162] *The Coming Struggle for Power*, John Strachey (Covici Friede, 1933) p. 359.
[163] JH unpublished article, HRC.
[164] Alec Waugh collection, HGARC.

a snow-covered Moscow. 'Moscow really strange',[165] Jack noted somewhat inadequately.

The two men stayed at the National Hotel on Mokhovaya Street, and, apart from a luncheon at the British Embassy, were escorted every step of the way by their Russian guide, a lugubrious middle-aged woman with an unchanging expression of boredom and distaste. The visitors were shown the main tourist sights – Red Square, the Kremlin, Lenin's tomb – and escorted round several model locations, a car factory, a juvenile prisoners' camp, a culture park and the newly built Moscow metro before beginning on their specifically designed itinerary. By arrangement with VOKS (the Committee for Cultural Relations) – 'actually, I was assured, a branch of OGPU [secret police]',[166] said Alec – they were allowed to hold a series of meetings with carefully selected painters and sculptors.

Jack, who was keen to understand the status of the artist under a communist regime, discussed fresco with the mural painter Vladimir Favorsky, and spent a morning with the three brothers Kukrinitzi, 'who draw and paint under one name, and who might be said to have realised the ideal of collective art'.[167]

The experience that impressed him most, however, was neither meeting contemporary Russian artists nor looking at their uniform style of social realism, but a visit to the State Museum of Western Art: here the scope and magnificence of the collections overwhelmed him. 'There are Cézannes, such as I never knew he painted. There are about twenty Gauguins more beautiful than I have ever seen in any other gallery or collection; Renoir is at his best; Van Gogh, Picasso in every period; and many, many others ...'[168]

When Jack returned from Mexico the year before, his political stance was on the far left, 'a near-communist', as he himself

---

[165] JH unpublished article, HRC.
[166] Alec Waugh collection, HGARC.
[167] JH unpublished article, HRC.
[168] Ibid.

described it. As with so many of his generation, Jack was appalled by much of what he saw in Britain of the 1930s; by the hunger marches, the living conditions of the unemployed, the indignities of the Means Test and by the glaring inequalities of the class system. Rivera had talked with enthusiasm of his experiences in Russia, and Jack had felt aligned with the growing left-wing movement that regarded Marxism and the Soviet Union as the model, the great white hope for the future.

Well before his visit to Moscow, he had joined a number of socialist organisations, most notably the Artists' International Association (AIA), the only overtly political organisation for artists in Britain. After his return he expanded his involvement, becoming a member of other progressive groups, such as the Society of Cultural Relations between the British Commonwealth and the USSR, for which he actively campaigned, making speeches, chairing meetings and entertaining fellow travellers, such as the singer Paul Robeson, who had visited the Soviet Union the previous year. And yet Jack was never wholly in love with 'the Scarlet Woman of the Steppes', and he had serious reservations about the communist model he had seen in Russia. The enforced conformity and terrifying penalties for dissent, the shocking poverty, squalor and drabness, as well as the general level of ignorance about the world outside, disturbed him deeply. When interviewed about his trip, he said with characteristic under-statement, 'I was somewhat disenchanted by my experience of the Soviet Union.'[169]

It was a few months after his return, in the autumn of 1935, that Jack undertook his first, and most overtly, political painting, a mural for the Karl Marx Memorial Library and Workers' School in Clerkenwell. The Marx Library, an eighteenth-century stucco building on Clerkenwell Green, is famous for its association with Lenin, who while in exile produced on its premises his samizdat journal, *Iskra*, which was then smuggled into Russia. The fresco,

---

[169] *Telegraph Magazine*, 18.1.81.

covering a wall in what was then the Lecture Hall on the first floor, was at first dully entitled *An Interpretation of Marxism*, later changed to the more dynamic, *The Worker of the Future Clearing away the Chaos of Capitalism*. In this painting the influence of Rivera is instantly apparent, in both subject and technique.

At the centre is the heroic figure of a bare-chested young man, broken shackles on his wrists and the rising sun behind him, powerfully symbolising the breaking by the worker of the chains of the capitalist state. As in Rivera's notorious mural in Rockefeller Center, the figure of Lenin is conspicuous on one side, here with Engels on his left, with on the other Karl Marx, Robert Owen and William Morris. In the forefront, watched by workers of the past and present, is a scene of violent destruction, churches, banks, the Stock Exchange, all tumbling into the abyss, with tiny figures running from the path of devastation, a peer in scarlet robes, a bishop, a society lady in a fur coat.

The mural for the Marx Library was the most challenging Jack had undertaken on his own, and it was fortunate that he had an assistant: his old friend Clifford Wight. Clifford had recently arrived in England after leaving the United States in something of a hurry. Shortly after the Hastingses arrived in Mexico, the Wights had moved to San Francisco, where, under the auspices of the Federal Works of Art Project, Clifford had been commissioned to paint four murals inside the Coit Memorial Tower.

Like Rivera before him, Clifford had been unable to resist introducing a couple of communist symbols, including the hammer and sickle, which when discovered naturally provoked an enraged reaction. The offending images were removed, and Clifford, by chance discovering he was about to be deported, was obliged to make a hasty departure, taking ship for England and giving Jack's St John's Wood address as his intended domicile. The two men were delighted to be reunited, and during the following weeks both fell easily into the old familiar Rivera-esque routine, starting work at 7.00 in the morning and continuing till nearly midnight until the job was done.

When completed, *The Worker of the Future* was admired by many visitors to the Marx Library, if it attracted little attention in the world outside. Some publicity was provided four years later when photographs of the mural were included in an exhibition at the Tate. Not long after this, however, it was decided at the Library that more wall-space was needed for books and so the fresco was covered in brown paper, bookshelves were placed against it, and there for over 40 years it stayed invisible and forgotten, until rediscovered in 1991, a year after the painter's death, and explored in a television documentary, *Marx on the Wall*.

In this, a number of distinguished academics give their opinion of the work and of its political significance. One describes it as a classical image of the socialism of a previous age, while another pertinently remarks on the striking absence of the all-powerful figure of Stalin; this, it is concluded, must be due to the influence of Rivera, whose deep hostility towards the Russian leader was well known. Perhaps the most eccentric comment came from the left-wing comedian Alexei Sayle, who saw the central figure of the bare-chested young man as homoerotic, 'like a boyfriend of W. H. Auden,'[170] he giggles, 'going off to the Café de Paris with Christopher Isherwood'.

During this period of the mid-1930s Jack undertook several other commissions for fresco: together with the designer Oliver Messel he decorated the interior of a fashionable new restaurant, Nerone, near Trafalgar Square; he painted a small mural in the house of Denis (D. N.) Pritt, the pro-Soviet barrister, depicting the return from Russia of the writer and artist, Pearl Binder; and completed another for his friend, John Betjeman, in his house at Uffington in Berkshire. ('Dearest Viscount,'[171] Betjeman wrote to him, 'I am enchanted ...') By far the most extensive project was a fresco for his old ally from Eton and Oxford, Gavin Henderson,

---

[170] *Marx on the Wall*. Bandung Ltd, 1991.
[171] HRC.

now Lord Faringdon, who had recently inherited a large estate, Buscot Park, in Oxfordshire.

Like Jack, Gavin had moved politically from right to far left, although with his camp voice and effeminate manner, few on first meeting would have seen in Gavin the dedicated and altruistic campaigner that lay behind the theatrical performance. In the park is an arched pavilion housing a small theatre, and it was on the walls and vaulting of the archway that Jack painted a series of pictures: Gavin addressing a political rally, Gavin with his guests at dinner, his friends playing tennis and swimming; also depicted are the work of the estate, with portraits of the farm manager and head gardener, and of various colleagues, his neighbour, Lord Berners, the Liberal politician, Violet Bonham-Carter, Gavin himself, Cristina and her sister-in-law Marian, and, most unusually, a self-portrait of the artist.

As the political situation continued to deteriorate, Jack wrote to his friend from Tahiti, Jimmy Hall, 'Conditions in Europe go from bad to worse. Fascism that inevitable prelude to war and destruction of all culture grows stronger daily & can, I think, only be counteracted by the voices of the left.'[172] He became increasingly involved in political activity, in 1935 helping to promote the first Congress of Peace and Friendship with the USSR, and also to organise an exhibition for the Artists' International Association in protest against Italy's invasion of Abyssinia. Entitled 'Artists Against War and Fascism' the show was held in a derelict building in Soho Square, attracting over 6,000 visitors, with works by, among others, Augustus John, Eric Ravilious, Barbara Hepworth and Henry Moore. Jack participated in other fund-raising events, chaired meetings at his St John's Wood house, hosted discussion panels, and appeared on the platform for the first meeting of the British Artists' Congress. This last event was denounced by the right-wing press as communist propaganda, a view clearly shared by MI5: from this time on and for some years to come both

---

[172] JH to James N. Hall 4.1.36. HRC.

Hastingses were kept under surveillance by British Intelligence as suspected communists and known agitators for a number of 'Comintern Front' organisations.

The political was the one territory on which the Hastingses were able to find common ground. When Jack began painting at the Karl Marx Library, Cristina also became involved, joining the General Committee and acting as Treasurer. Now she took a step further to the left, for it was during this period that she became a member of the Communist Party. Like her husband, Cristina had been powerfully influenced by the political convictions of the Riveras, and since returning to England had experienced few of the doubts and reservations that had afflicted Jack.

Now as a comrade, she had found a sense of belonging, her passionate, unphilosophical nature focusing on a cause to which she was able to dedicate herself with almost fanatical fervour, and to which she was to remain committed for the rest of her life. It was at this period, shortly after joining the Party, that she embarked on a rash adventure which was to land her in serious trouble.

The only member of Jack's family to whom Cristina had always been close was his youngest sister. Marian, a recent widow after her husband's death from tuberculosis, had from their first meeting been immediately captivated by Cristina, the two women forming an affectionate alliance, keeping regularly in touch while on opposite sides of the globe. Marian had spent a considerable time in South America while she and Patrick had been based in the Falklands, and thus her sudden decision to collaborate with Cristina on a travel book about Brazil was received with less surprise than it might have been. Oddly, no one thought to comment on the fact that the country's notoriously repressive fascist regime hardly made it the safest place for a visiting communist.

Marian and Cristina set sail in February 1936. As soon as they arrived in Rio de Janeiro, the ship was boarded by armed police who escorted the two women off for a session of intensive interrogation, warning them they would be kept under 24-hour surveillance until their departure. A few days later, while on a visit to São Paulo, they were arrested as they left their hotel and held for over eight hours in jail until finally released after the personal intervention of the British Ambassador. In a newspaper interview, Cristina expressed outrage at her treatment: she described as scandalous the accusation that she, Viscountess Hastings, an innocent travel writer, had been trying to smuggle in letters to communists and other political prisoners. 'We had not realised',[173] said Cristina proudly, 'the terror the Brazilian Government has of authors.' In fact, as was later revealed in a series of communiqués intercepted by MI5, the British visitors had been attempting to discover the whereabouts of Luis Prestos, the communist revolutionary who had recently 'disappeared' under President Vargas's fascist regime.

Relieved though he was that Cristina's escapade had ended without further incident, Jack had little reason to look forward to her return. On the domestic front their relations continued profoundly unhappy. To his sister Norah, Jack confided that his domestic existence had become unbearable, that it was now 'Hell, with a big H', with Cristina creating one storm after another from morning to night; he recognised that his wife, 'with her excitable temperament just can't help it', yet that made it no easier to bear. Equally frustrating for Cristina was her husband's impenetrable reserve: the more she raged the more silent and withdrawn he became, a lack of response that then provoked her to further emotionally violent attacks. Fortunately, the Hastingses were not to stay under the same roof for much longer.

Less than six months after Cristina returned from Brazil, Jack left for Spain. The Spanish Civil War had broken out in July 1936, and although of little concern to many in Britain – 'just a lot of bloody dagoes killing each other',[174] in the words of Randolph Churchill – for those on the left the war was of sinister significance. The fact that the British government was continuing to

[173] *Sunday Dispatch*, 29.3.36.
[174] *British Women and the Spanish Civil War*, Angela Jackson (Routledge, 2002) p. 5.

maintain a position of non-intervention, despite evidence that the Nationalists were receiving substantial support from Italy and Nazi Germany, was giving rise to increasing alarm as the forces of fascism grew more powerful by the day.

With Jack in the small cross-party delegation that arrived in Spain at the beginning of September were two Labour MPs, Seymour Cocks and William Dobbie, and the communist Isabel Brown, one of the founders of the recently formed Spanish Medical Aid Committee. On the track of first-hand information, they travelled to Barcelona, Valencia, Toledo and Madrid, holding interviews with provincial governors and members of the military, as well as with Manuel Azaña, President of the Republic. They also collected more tangible indications of foreign intervention, including an Italian parachute and photographs of a captured German aeroplane, 'ample evidence', as Jack wrote in a letter to the *Morning Post*, 'that supplies of arms have been given to the rebels by the Fascist countries'.

More revealing than this factual statement, however, were the photographs Jack brought back with him, pictures of Toledo bombarded and Alcazar under siege, of Republican soldiers standing at ease, of assault guards cheerfully picnicking by the roadside, of a group of International Brigaders enjoying a joke. And shortly after his return he painted a strikingly telling picture, a fresco of Spanish Government Militia on the march; painted on a portable metal panel it was shown at the Lefevre Galleries in Mayfair in December 1936 but has since disappeared.

The show at the Lefevre was Jack's first solo exhibition in London, the private view attended by such well-known figures as H. G. Wells, Osbert Sitwell and Somerset Maugham, as well as a number of friends from Jack's bachelor days, among them Evan Tredegar and Alice Wimborne. The exhibition attracted little attention from the critics – a polite nod in *The Times*, a dismissive few lines from Clive Bell in the *New Statesman* – although there was one encouraging review by the distinguished art historian (and, it should be noted, crypto-communist), Anthony Blunt.

Beginning by informing his readers that Hastings was a pupil of Diego Rivera, Blunt goes on to praise the artist's sensitivity and powers of observation, his sense of colour, and 'the superb and not altogether kind realism of some of the portraits';[175] if he can keep up the qualities here on display, Blunt concludes, 'he will become the English Rivera, not in the sense of the English follower, but the English equivalent'.

Blunt's comment about the 'not altogether kind realism' is particularly relevant in three remarkable portraits of this period: of the actress Flora Robson, pale and austere; of his sister Kathleen's husband, Bunkie Curzon-Herrick, in all his fat-faced, benign stupidity; and, most striking of all, of Jack's mother-in-law, the Marchesa Casati. In Jack's painting Luisa is not the exotic, flame-haired beauty so often portrayed in the past, but a gaunt, middle-aged woman in a plain black hat; the large kohl-rimmed eyes look warily out from behind a short veil; round her neck, like a yoke, is a massive leopard-skin collar; and in her right hand she holds a crystal ball, perhaps a reference to the extreme unpredictability of her future. Describing the portrait, French *Vogue* commented, 'derrière sa voilette, son regard est celui d'une sorcière légèrement abrutie'.[176]

Over the past few years the Marchesa's fortunes had altered dramatically. In 1931, after a lifetime of spending without restraint, Luisa had found herself bankrupt, over $24 million in debt. Destitute, she had moved to London, to a tiny flat in Beaufort Gardens, off the Brompton Road, where she lived off the charity of a group of friends, among them Gavin Faringdon, Evan Tredegar, Naps Alington, Augustus John and, after his return from abroad, her son-in-law, Jack. Serenely solipsistic, Luisa seemed little concerned by the change in her fortunes. Her monthly allowance was spent within hours, and Luisa became adept at writing pathetic letters to her band of providers. The only

---

[175] *Spectator*, 18.12.36.
[176] 'behind her veil, her look is that of a witch slightly dazed ...'

surviving letter of hers to Jack is just such a plea for an increase in funds. 'Cher Jack, Je vous écris seulement pour vous demander si vous pourriez m'aider un peu dans un moment très difficile … ma situation est très sérieuse et je m'adresse à vous ayant toujours gardé un souvenir très sympathique de vous et sachant que vous comprenez les situations compliqués.'[177]

Over time her witch-like figure became a familiar sight in Chelsea, dressed in a shabby black coat with monkey-fur collar, accompanied by her Pekinese, Spider. She always wore a coal-scuttle hat and dark glasses, these to conceal the fact that her eyes had turned scarlet from regular use over years of belladonna to enlarge the pupils. Never without friends, she accepted every invitation, and appeared to adapt to her new life with remarkable ease, her relations with her daughter remaining as benign and indifferent as they had been in Cristina's childhood.

Soon after his exhibition at the Lefevre had closed, Jack returned again to Spain. This time he went out under the aegis of Spanish Medical Aid, his primary mission the inspection of field hospitals, to assess how best the meagre funding should be spent. His secondary purpose, but to him of overwhelming importance, was to investigate the precautions taken to protect the nation's works of art. As a member of the Artists' International Association, Jack had been much involved in raising funds for beleaguered artists in Spain; he was also to stand as patron and guarantor when in 1938 Picasso's *Guernica*, his famous painting of the Spanish Civil War, arrived to go on show in London. Now, on this second trip, he wanted to see for himself what measures had been taken to protect the national collections. Of particular concern, during the bombing raids on Madrid, had been the contents of the Prado, most of which had been removed to secure premises in Valencia.

Here Jack was allowed to inspect the secret location, an enormous stone vault with iron and asbestos doors, in which

---

[177] 'Dear Jack, I am writing to ask if you could help me at a very difficult time … my situation is very serious and I'm turning to you having always remembered you as most sympathetic and knowing that you understand difficult situations.'

were stored large, well-ventilated wooden cases. 'One enormous case contained Titian's "Equestrian Portrait of Charles V", a small heavy box had the original plates of Goya's "Disasters of the War" … Other cases were filled with El Grecos, Goyas, Titians, Rubens, and Velasquez.' The ventilation was well controlled, sentries were always on guard, and, he reported, 'the Spanish Government are taking every possible care of the artistic patrimony of their country'.

It was when on his way back from this second journey to Spain that by chance Jack's final disillusionment with communism occurred. His experience of Soviet Russia had made him uneasy, but now while spending the night in a cheap hotel in Paris he overheard through the thin walls of his bedroom a couple of Comintern agents discussing with callous cynicism how success-fully they had manipulated the British delegates. As for many of Jack's compatriots in Spain, George Orwell among them, it came as a shock to learn of the ruthlessness of Soviet communism, that Stalin's support for the Republican side, while masquerading as anti-fascism, was driven solely by the desire to promote Soviet interests and to take eventual control of the Republic.

It was largely as a result of this revelation that from now Jack began to move away from his position as fellow traveller with the Party. 'Although I remained Labour, I wasn't so left after that,'[178] he remarked many years later in an interview.

No such doubts about communist policy assailed Cristina. On joining the Party she had immediately become involved with the Spanish Medical Aid Committee (SMAC), being appointed one of two treasurers. The other was Viscount Churchill, cousin of Winston, and a notoriously raffish character. Described by one his colleagues as 'wildly homosexual, financially dishonest, *most* charming',[179] Peter Churchill was an old friend of Jack's. The two of them had been together on Jack's first visit to Madrid, combining

---

[178] *Telegraph Magazine*, 18.1.81.
[179] *The Impact of the Spanish Civil War on Britain: War, Loss and Memory*, Tom Buchanan (Sussex Academic Press, 2006).

to conduct interviews with various military commanders; like many of the foreign correspondents they had stayed at the Hotel Florida where, as Peter recalled, 'the chambermaid kept everything on her floor looking most elegant, though the end of the corridor was blasted, and from it you could see half across Madrid'.[180]

In March 1937 Cristina left for Spain, with Peter and other members of the British section of SMAC. As a companion Peter proved exceptionally sympathetic and he and Cristina quickly struck up a friendship. When the two of them finally reached the SMAC headquarters in Valencia, one of the delegates was struck by the incongruous elegance of the new arrivals, 'an English peer, who might have come straight from Pall Mall, and an Anglo-Italian peeress, who might have come straight from the Lido'.[181]

During those first weeks in Spain Peter and Cristina were constantly in each other's company, touring field hospitals, organising the small detachments of volunteer nurses, driving ambulances, and for Cristina the job of interviewing Italian prisoners of war. As she reported to Jack, '300 soldiers & four officers. You can imagine what a lot of talking there was. Me and that many Italians!' After a while, however, Peter faded from the scene, intent on pursuing a relationship with a good-looking young interpreter, and it was at this point that Cristina met another aristocratic young Englishman, who was shortly to change the course of her life.

Wogan Philipps, handsome, excitable, was, like Jack, a rebel against a conventional, right-wing background. His wealthy father, Lord Milford, was in the shipping business, but Wogan had no interest in such a career, defying his family by becoming a painter, a pursuit for which he showed more enthusiasm than talent. In 1928 he had married the novelist Rosamond Lehmann, but they had not proved compatible, both conducting adulterous affairs while never quite reaching the point of divorce. Wogan, like Cristina a recent member of the Party, had immediately volunteered for

---

[180] *All My Sins Remembered*, Viscount Churchill (Heinemann 1964) p. 171.
[181] *A Theory of My Time: an Essay in Didactic Reminiscence*, Richard Rees (Secker & Warburg, 1963).

Spain on the outbreak of war, driving an ambulance and coura-
geously acting as medical assistant during the terrible Battle of
Jarama.

After their first meeting, he and Cristina soon found they had
a great deal in common: both passionately committed to the
Republican cause, both emotional, unintellectual and outspoken,
both unhappily married. When Cristina eventually returned to
England, Wogan, still in Spain, asked her to call on his wife,
Rosamond, and give her news of him. Obligingly Cristina drove
down to Oxfordshire, but the moment she appeared Rosamond's
suspicions were aroused. 'I knew the moment I saw her',[182] she
said. 'I sensed that she'd got her claws into Wogan ... She was very
friendly, full of passionate pro-International Brigade propaganda,
exactly the sort of thing Wogan would swallow hook, line and
sinker. But I suspected she was in love with him.'

Predictably, the reaction from Burton to the Hastingses political
activities had been one of outrage. Socialism, communism, all
were anathema to the Huntingdons. When Jack went to Russia
Maud had been '*alarmed* & *horrified*': Bolsheviks were the spawn
of Satan (she knew for a fact they were plotting to divert the Gulf
Stream) and those Reds were worse than wild beasts, horrible,
conscienceless *scum*. As usual her daughter-in-law received most
of the blame. When Jack left on his first mission to Spain, Maud
wrote to Cristina,

> To run into a country *seething* with red *revolution* is the *acme* of folly
> ... I really can't think Jack would have taken such an insane step
> had he not been *worked up* to it by someone. & I am afraid it won't
> be hard to guess who the someone is ... Why don't you go *yourself*
> Cristina, if you care so much about it all, & see what those *devils* can
> do to poor suffering humanity.

After Jack returned a few weeks later, his mother immediately
turned her fire on him, denouncing him for taking part in this

---

[182] *Rosamond Lehmann*, Selina Hastings (Chatto & Windus, 2002) p. 186.

'very reckless & foolhardy *expedition* … I wish you'd leave politics *severely alone*,' she continued. 'Stick to your painting it is much safer – & if Cristina is so fond of the Bolsheviks why does she not go & *live* among them.'

Meanwhile, the war between Jack and his parents over Moorea had escalated sharply. While Cristina was away, Jack had visited Burton fairly regularly to see his daughter, even writing to her from time to time in his illegible hand and sending her presents: a penknife, a pedometer, on her birthdays a cake and a £5 note. Emotionally unengaged he may have been, but he wanted to do what he believed was best for her. Clearly she was learning little from the relaxed regime at Dartington, and both he and Cristina agreed that she should be sent to school in Switzerland where she would learn good French and receive a more cosmopolitan education. Although initially daunted, Moorea on arrival in Nyon quickly adapted to her new environment: she made friends with the other English girls, who admired her horsemanship, and soon became expert at skating and skiing. 'I enjoyed it,' she said looking back. 'The girls were friendly, the teachers kind, and after the first few days I never felt homesick at all.'

None of this impressed Maud, who from the beginning had been vehemently opposed to the project. 'Girls learn *fifty times more* from a good governess than at *any* school … To pack that little girl off to a *foreign country* among *complete* strangers is cruel & unkind … It is like throwing a lily in the mud … To learn a *smattering* of *vile Swiss* French won't compensate for all the *harm* you are doing.' As usual it was Cristina's fault, and as usual Maud had no hesitation in speaking her mind. 'She is *universally detested … disliked* by *everyone*, & you can tell her so,' wrote Maud. 'I don't wish to see C. darken my doors for some time to come.'

It was beyond Maud's comprehension how Jack could prefer to place himself 'under the thumb of this *unpleasant individual* & do *all* she wishes instead of trying to please your parents'. If this to Jack sounded like the usual rant then he failed to understand how serious this was, although the message was clear enough. 'You have *lost* a *great deal already* Jack through Cristina's *extravagance, stupidity & tactlessness*', his mother warned him. 'Take care you don't lose a great deal *more* than you have any *idea* of.'

Up to now it had always been Maud who engaged in battle; it was she who appeared to control almost everything, with Warner concerning himself only with his horses and the hunt. This time, however, it was different. Warner, who normally preferred to stay out of family quarrels – 'anything for a quiet life' was a favourite saying of his – now took over. He dearly loved his little grand-daughter and had finally come to the end of his patience with his son. 'My dear Jack,' he wrote. 'No use wasting words or time & am sick of useless arguments.' All this nonsense about sending Moorea to school abroad must stop, he continued; she must live at Burton to be properly brought up and educated by a governess.

> You can come & see her any time you wish. Now this is a simple business proposition & just requires an answer yes or no. Mr White is coming down to make our wills & on your reply to this offer depends what we put in them … We have made up our minds about things & as we both have a good bit to leave (to whom we like) it might be well to consider what you are going to do … Excuse short letter but I am finished with arguments.

But if Warner were implacable, so was Jack. The threat could not have been plainer, yet Jack refused to comply. And when Warner died two years later it was found he had been true to his word: he left not a penny to his only son.

On 19 May 1937, while Cristina was still in Spain, Jack attended a party given by Alec Waugh in the River Room at the Savoy. Late that same evening a party in another London hotel was just coming to an end, a dinner in Victorian costume organised by the fashion historian, Doris Langley-Moore. By the entrance to the cloakroom an attractive young couple, both in nineteenth-century dress, were waiting to collect their coats. Bryan Wallace, son of the thriller-writer Edgar Wallace, was in the film business; his wife, Margaret Lane, a novelist and journalist.

While waiting their turn, Margaret idly listened to the squabbling of the pair in front. '*Why* can't you take me?' the girl was demanding. 'It'll be fun and I want to go.' 'You weren't invited and that's an end of the matter,' her companion firmly replied. Suddenly Margaret realised what they were talking about: Alec's party, which she and Bryan had promised to attend. 'Oh, I *can't*,' said Bryan. 'I'm too tired, and I have to be at the studio early in the morning. But why don't you go?' So she did. And it was there that Alec introduced Margaret to Jack; he asked her to dance and during the course of the evening began to fall in love with her.

By the time Cristina returned to London the following month, the affair was well under away. Already Jack knew what he wanted: divorce from his wife and to marry Margaret, not the least of whose attractions was her complete antithesis to Cristina. Strikingly pretty in a very English way, with short wavy brown hair and large grey-blue eyes, Margaret was clever, witty, and remarkably even-tempered. The only obstacle between them was Margaret's fondness for her husband, to whom she had been married for only three years, an amicable rather than passionate relationship, but one which she was reluctant to destroy.

Bryan, currently working as scriptwriter for Alexander Korda at London Films, had a little house in Bloomfield Terrace, off Sloane Square, where the Wallaces spent the week, with weekends in a cottage in Hampshire. Their professional lives were complex and busy, Bryan at the call of the studio, while Margaret, a star reporter for the *Daily Mail* – in those days a sober and responsible newspaper – was also the author of a prize-winning novel and shortly to publish a biography of her father-in-law, Edgar Wallace.

As the weeks passed of furtive telephone calls and secret meetings, it soon became clear to both Jack and Margaret that they must be together, whatever the consequences. Bryan, after the initial shock, was understanding and agreed to begin the lengthy process of divorcing his wife, with Margaret, as required, to be discovered as the guilty party. But for Jack the situation was far more complex.

After Cristina returned from Spain Jack braced himself to talk to her. She had known nothing of the relationship and was utterly distraught; furious, she refused even to discuss the question of divorce. But Jack was determined, and this time he had ammunition of his own: he told her that unless she agreed, he would bring a suit against her on the evidence of her adultery with Wogan Philipps. Cristina was devastated. There was no denying her affair with Wogan, which was continuing, and yet she wanted to remain married to Jack, the love of her life. Now her only hope was to delay and to make difficulties in the hope that he would come to his senses, tire of Margaret and eventually return to her.

And thus began several years of miserable wrangling, with Cristina desperately struggling to hold on to her husband while he with equal determination fought to be free. Acting as arbitrator during much of this period was Jack's sister, Norah, who although wholly on her brother's side, was acutely aware of Cristina's unhappiness. '[Jack] is *madly* in love at the moment,' Norah wrote to her parents. 'He writes to me that nothing on earth would induce him ever to go back to Cristina … No nerves could stand that for ever, and I suppose in comparison the other appears a haven of peace and rest.'

To Cristina herself Norah showed genuine sympathy, while at the same time trying to persuade her to accept the irrevocable. 'I hate to think of all the unhappiness you are going through,' Norah told her, '[but] all the sympathy in the world won't alter facts … I am sure that you have loved – and still do love – Jack more than anyone has, and nobody can ever take away the happiness you and he have had together … but you know Jack well enough to realise how determined he can be on any subject once his mind is made up.'

In her last paragraph Norah refers approvingly to a recent suggestion of Cristina's. 'I think the plan you speak of in your letter of possibly going to America for a bit, seems a good one.' This decision was arrived at shortly after Jack, too, had made up his mind to leave the country: in September 1938 he and Margaret went to the west of Ireland, where in a small cottage on the beautiful coast of Galway the two of them were able to live peacefully while the tortuous process of separation rumbled on.

Cristina, meanwhile, was rescued by her old friend, Alice von Hofmannstahl, who owned a magnificent house on the Hudson in upstate New York; here at Rhinebeck Cristina, accompanied by her 12-year-old daughter, settled in for a prolonged stay. Alice, kind and gentle, provided a welcome retreat, doing her best to comfort Cristina and immediately accepting Moorea as one of the family. For Moorea staying at Rhinebeck was the highlight of her early years: she never forgot Alice's warmth and generosity, the days spent skating on the Hudson and playing with Alice's children, the excitement of occasional trips to New York for shopping and the theatre.

In February 1939 Bryan Wallace was granted a decree nisi. Two months later, on 5 April, Warner Huntingdon died. His funeral was held in the Hastings chapel of St Helen's Church at Ashby-de-la-Zouch in Leicestershire, the mourners led by his widow and by his only son, now the 16th Earl of Huntingdon. Many were the respectful obituaries, typical among them an article in *The Times*, which described the deceased peer as 'a keen judge of a working hound ... Never beaten, out of heart, or out of temper, he was universally respected and beloved in the hunting field.'[183] It was left to a local paper, the *Loughborough Monitor*, to look into the future; regarding the political stance of the new Earl, it nervously enquired whether 'the distinction of being connected with the first Communist Member of the House of Lords may fall to Loughborough'.[184]

For the next nearly four years Jack and Margaret lived quietly together, first in Ireland, then in England where they returned just before the outbreak of war. Here they spent most of their time in the cottage in Hampshire which Margaret had once shared with

---

[183] *The Times*, 6.4.39.
[184] *Loughborough Monitor & Herald*, 27.4.39.

Bryan, Margaret working on a new novel, Jack painting and acting as an ARP (Air Raids Precautions) officer for Andover District Council, with occasional forays up to London to see his lawyers and to attend the House of Lords.

Finally, the divorce from Cristina came through, awarding her custody of Moorea. On 1 February 1944, only weeks before Cristina became the wife of Wogan Philipps, Jack and Margaret were married at St Pancras Registry Office, their honeymoon five luxurious days at Claridge's Hotel. At the beginning of the following year, they moved from Hampshire to the village of Forston in Dorset, to a beautiful grey-stone house which by chance had belonged to Alice von Hofmannstahl. 'I forget if I have told you that we think that we have at last found a very nice house', Jack wrote to his sister Norah. 'I heard of it through an agent and was half way round inspecting it when I thought that I recognised some of the pictures and furniture, and we discovered that it belonged to Alice ... A most extraordinary coincidence ... It was built about 1740 and has a small trout stream at the bottom of the garden ...'

10

The Invisible Man

After the turbulent years with Cristina, it must have been a relief for my father to settle down to a relatively peaceful way of life. He and my mother proved remarkably compatible; he had his painting, she her writing, and they always seemed able to do very much as they pleased. They travelled widely, bought houses here and there, including one for a time on Elba, another in Morocco, and devoted much of the summer to sailing, my father keeping a yacht, *Sharavogue*, on the Beaulieu River. They had a wide circle of friends, mainly in the arts and in politics, including many whom my father had known at Eton and Oxford. During the period when he first started living with my mother, he owed his financial independence to Maud. Despite the years of disobedience and revolt, Maud could not bring herself to abandon her son, and after Warner cut Jack out of his will, Maud, now the Dowager, made it up to him from money she had recently inherited from one of her brothers. So relieved was she that Cristina was at last out of the picture that she made a conscious effort to be civil to Margaret, despite the obvious unsuitability of this middle-class divorcée as the new Countess of Huntingdon.

Even so, the semi-annual visits to Burton were dreaded by my mother, who knew nothing of hunting and had little interest in county society. She was fascinated by Maud as a character, however, and relished the acerbic flavour of her mother-in-law's outspokenness. One day, as my grandmother was making her way slowly down the front steps, about to be eased into the car by her chauffeur, she sneezed violently. 'Oh, Lady Huntingdon, I do hope you haven't caught cold,' said my mother politely. 'Yes, I have,' Maud crossly replied. 'My *stupid* maid put me into a cold fur-coat!' All the servants were spoken to with a directness that often shocked newcomers to the house. When Maud, as she frequently did, mislaid her handbag she often accused her saintly and long-suffering butler, William Griffin, of stealing it. 'You'll end up in prison one of these days,' she warned him. 'There are worse places than prison, m'lady,' replied William wearily, retrieving the bag from its usual place beside her armchair.

I vividly remember my grandmother and visiting Burton in the years just after the war. By then Maud was approaching 80, a small, stout figure, with grey hair and, like Queen Mary, a false front of grey curls. Right up to her death at the age of 85 she continued to entertain, giving elaborate luncheons and dinners, to which, according to my mother, 'every crashing bore in Leicestershire was sure to be invited'. In summer she organised charity fêtes in the garden, and every Christmas threw a lavish party for the children of the local gentry, with a huge tree and piles of presents distributed by a scarlet-coated Santa Claus.

During our visits, my sister Caroline and I were billeted in the nursery, from where, true to tradition, we were brought down every afternoon at 5.00 p.m., in tidy frocks, our hair neatly brushed, to be received in the library by our grandmother. We always found her sitting by the fire, and the form was that we were to search for the sweeties she had hidden about the room. This was good fun, particularly as they were never difficult to find, positioned rather obviously, and at exactly our height, on top of the rows of bound copies of *Punch* and *Baily's Hunting Directory*.

Her passion for the theatre undimmed, Maud took us to the pantomime in Leicester, where I vaguely remember seeing George Formby and his ukulele, and in 1948 to the Shakespeare Memorial Theatre at Stratford, where our 20-year-old half-sister Moorea was playing Mama Rabbit in a production of *Toad of Toad Hall*. This was Moorea's first professional engagement, her first experience of an independent existence. After her parents separated, she had spent her holidays with her mother on Wogan Philipp's farm in

Gloucestershire, interspersed with visits to Burton and to Jack and Margaret at their cottage in Hampshire.

Wogan was an amiable step-father, and Moorea became fond of him, and of Hugo and Sally, his two children by Rosamond Lehmann, grateful for the protection they provided from Cristina's unstable temperament. Finally, at 18, Moorea struck out on her own with a brief career on the stage, of which the highlight was playing Emilia in Orson Welles's 1951 production of *Othello*. During these years Moorea remained an unknown quantity to Caroline and me, and I have no recollection of ever being in her company.

The next time I remember her was in 1957, on the occasion of her wedding to the Labour politician, Woodrow Wyatt. The reception was on the terrace of the House of Lords, and Moorea appeared a dazzling figure, transformed from the plump teenager I had seen in photographs to a slender, smiling beauty dressed in elegant couture.

Moorea's wedding took place four years after the death of her mother. Despite their shared commitment to communism, Cristina's marriage to Wogan had not been happy, Wogan, like my father, coming to dread his wife's 'foul temper'.[185] Their strongest bond was political: in a letter to the communist campaigner, Harry Pollitt, Wogan wrote that it was Cristina who 'rescued me from being a hopeless dilettante, and brought me firmly into the Party'.[186]

After the death in 1947 of her father, Camillo Casati, Cristina was left a substantial legacy, including a share in the family palazzo in Milan, where she increasingly spent time, often on her own and usually on Party business. In 1950 Wogan began an affair with a Russian communist, Tamara Rust, widow of Bill Rust, editor of the *Daily Worker*, and before long the two decided to marry. However, Wogan postponed his plans for divorce after Cristina fell ill with cancer, from which she died on 22 March 1953. On the

---

[185] Wogan Philipps to Tamara Rust 1947. 'England's Rivera: the Lost Murals of Viscount John Hastings 1931–1938'. Alison Maclean.
[186] Wogan Philipps to Harry Pollitt, ibid.

day of her death Wogan, reportedly at Tamara's instigation, threw all Cristina's papers, a lifetime's carefully preserved collection of letters, photographs and a drafted memoir, into the river.

There is no record of how Luisa, who survived her daughter by four years, reacted to Cristina's death. I remember once asking my father what this legendary figure, the Marchesa Casati, had been like. He thought for a moment and then said reflectively, 'Rather difficult as a mother-in-law.' And that was that.

My father meanwhile had continued to pursue a political career, taking his seat on the Labour benches in the House of Lords. At the beginning of the war he had vigorously campaigned for independence for India, in 1942 writing a slim volume on the subject, his first (and last) publication since *The Golden Octopus* in 1928. For five years, from 1945 to 1950, he served in Clement Attlee's government, appointed, in tandem with the future Foreign Secretary, George Brown, to the Ministry of Agriculture and Fisheries. Years later I met George Brown and asked him if he remembered my father. 'Oh, yes,' he replied. 'Jack was charming, but our Minister was one of those men who couldn't delegate, had to do everything himself, so life in the office was very boring. I tried to get Jack to support me in demanding more work – but you know, for some reason he never would.'

In November 1950 Jack resigned. 'Five years of that was enough for me,' he said in an interview. 'I didn't like having to give up painting.' Yet he continued regularly to attend Parliament, actively supporting favoured causes such as the abolition of capital punishment, nuclear disarmament, and in 1967 the repeal of the Criminal Law Amendment Act (more informally known as homosexual law reform). Ten years earlier there had been a brief return to his communistic past when he and my mother and their old friend Graham Greene, as part of a small delegation of writers and artists, took off for China at the personal invitation of Chairman Mao. In his later years my father moved slightly further towards the centre, although his sympathies remained always with the Labour Party.

Yet despite his leftist leanings, my father had great respect for history and tradition. In 1953 he and my mother in full rig attended the coronation of Elizabeth II. About to put on the heavy scarlet robes, Jack noticed something not quite right about the ermine cape, and then he remembered: years ago at Sharavogue Maud had had it cut off to make an evening cloak, replacing the expensive ermine with rabbit.

In a letter from the 1970s to Alec Waugh, Jack wrote, 'More and more I am convinced that creative people should not retire while they can still wield pen, brush or chisel',[187] and it is in his studio that over time I see my father most clearly. Here he would spend hours painting or drawing, dressed in an old grey overall or a shabby blue denim jacket bought years ago in Mexico City. The room smelt enticingly of turpentine and paint and linseed oil; there was an easel, and an architect's chest where he kept his drawings, bookshelves, and a table on which sat a pewter jar full of brushes; on one wall was a lithograph of Rivera's nude portrait of Frida, and over the fireplace a reproduction of Gauguin's *Arearea*.

A little Mexican idol stood on his desk, on the window-sill a collection of shells from the South Seas, and in one corner a Huntley & Palmer's biscuit tin filled with sand in which were a collection of Indian arrows brought back from California. Attractive young women, nurses mostly, would come to the house at intervals to sit for him. Occasionally he asked my sister and me to oblige. Most children would have dreaded such periods of immobility but for me, lazy by nature, these sessions were entirely agreeable: I would happily sit for 40 minutes or an hour, staring into space, thinking of nothing in particular, music from the radio in the background and my father at his easel drawing with great concentration.

Fresco remained his chief interest, and for this he always acknowledged the great debt he owed to Rivera. During his brief

---

[187] JH to Alec Waugh 6.9.74. Alec Waugh collection, HGARC.

period as a student at the Slade, Jack had been taught by Henry Tonks, known for his advocacy of mural decoration, but when the subject arose he always insisted it was not Tonks but Diego who had provided his inspiration. Jack was an early member of the Society of Mural Painters, and for a brief period he taught fresco, first at Camberwell School of Arts, later, in the early 1950s, at the Central St Martin's School of Art. Over the years there were a few exhibitions, and occasionally my father undertook a commission, a fresco for Birmingham University, another for the Women's Press Club off Fleet Street, several in private houses for friends. But for us, his family, by far the most exciting was a mural he painted on all four walls in the breakfast-room of our house in London. This was a dramatic and vibrant jungle scene, full of cannibals, spears and skulls, luxuriant Rivera-esque foliage, and the snarling head of a tiger, modelled on the Esso advertisement then current, with its famous slogan, 'Put a tiger in your tank!'

Shortly after this painting was finished my father decided to try his hand at mosaic, and it was now that Clifford Wight appeared on the scene. We knew he was an old friend, but other than that my father had told us little about him. Gaunt, grey-haired, still very handsome, Clifford arrived with a plump, pretty girlfriend, Connie, a potter: he and Jean had divorced some years earlier, and Clifford, after a short stint teaching fresco at Central St Martin's, had retired to the country where he lived in a village near Cheltenham.

Dozens of bags of little stones were delivered to the house, and Caroline and I were given the job of sorting the colours into separate piles, an entertaining occupation for about five minutes, after which it quickly palled. The only finished result was a small mosaic of a snail, after which the exercise was abandoned, Clifford and my father turning their attention first to engraving, then to a design for a funerary urn, destined eventually to hold Jack's ashes in the Hastings chapel at Ashby-de-la-Zouch.

In many areas my father remained a mystery to his children, which is strange in a way for he was a mesmerising story-teller. When we were small he would often come upstairs to say goodnight, sitting at the end of our beds and holding us enthralled with exciting and often terrifying tales, the origins of which I was later to discover in *The Lost World*, *King Solomon's Mines* and *The Monkey's Paw*. Only occasionally did he talk about his own past, about Australia and Tahiti and Mexico, and a man called Diego, although for a long time we had no idea who Diego was.

A favourite subject was his famous forebear, Robin Hood, whose creed he clearly admired. '[Robin Hood] stood for social justice,'[188] he wrote in an article, '[for] the liberty of the individual and for the recognition of the rights of the people against the oppression of their masters.' Like his ancestor, my father was an excellent shot with bow and arrow and tried to teach my sister and me, but we proved inept as archers and he gave up after Caroline one day shot our pony. Silver, enjoying a peaceful retirement in the field next to the garden, had strolled out from a small grove of trees just as my sister was taking aim. The arrow hit her flank, but fortunately she never noticed, never even looked up, and the arrow bounced off with no harm done. In 1965 Jack was presented with the opportunity of encountering Robin Hood on the West End stage, in a musical by Lionel Bart jauntily entitled *Twang!!* He and the Sheriff of Nottingham were invited to the first night, but as the evening approached my father found he couldn't face it and sent me in his stead. All I remember was that the show was so under-rehearsed the cast had to read their lines off the trees in Sherwood Forest, and the Sheriff of Nottingham left abruptly in the interval.

Gradually as I came to know him a little, I began to understand what a complicated character my father was. One of his lovers, with whom he had an affair shortly before he met my mother, accurately described his impenetrable nature. 'I have never known how you felt,' she complained. 'There seems to be a little curtain in front of you which I have never been able to penetrate.' Certainly he was generous and good-natured, but also expert at emotional concealment.

---

[188] JH unpublished article, HRC.

In an article written after his death, he was described as 'full
of kindness and amusing stories ... vague, gentle, courteous, and
charming, with exquisite manners [which were] sometimes taken
for weakness, but he was politely resolute in avoiding inconven-
ience to himself.'[189] This latter statement was certainly true: my
father, like his father before him, rarely did anything against his
will, and for all his gentleness he had an inflexible streak which
enabled him nearly always to have his own way.

He seldom lost his temper, about once every three years on
average, but when he did it was impossibly difficult to deal with.
Instead of raising his voice he would retreat into an icy tundra of
remoteness, and there he would stay, sometimes for days, until
the thaw set in. 'There's nothing to do but wait it out,' my mother
would say resignedly.

My father died in 1990, at the age of 89. I would give anything
to have him back, even if only for 24 hours so that I could hear
the rest of the story, for there is more still to be told. When shortly
after his death I was going through the papers stored in his studio
I came across the following, completely mystifying, typewritten
note. '*The Secret: an Autobiography Not to be revealed till 1990*:
For some time my wife and more especially my daughters have
been urging me to write my autobiography. The real reason for
my reluctance I have never disclosed; I will call it 'the secret'. It all
started in such an innocent and simple way. A strange meeting
in Paris, knowing Edwina well many years ago (I have destroyed
all her letters except one harmless one), being given a lift home
by Stafford Cripps when I was Parliamentary Secretary in the
Ministry of Agriculture, and a walk down Jermyn Street after
midnight. And of course the accidental meeting of the real and
important participants in the most extraordinary circumstances.'

What any of this refers to I have no idea. Certainly my father
knew Edwina Mountbatten, part of the social circle in which he

---

[189] Woodrow Wyatt. *Oxford Dictionary of National Biography* (Oxford University
Press, 2004).

moved in the 1920s. When I looked through his papers I did indeed find a note from Edwina, which from the address must have been written well before the war. 'Dear Jack, Thank you for your letter and it was nice of you to write. I really think we had better leave matters as they are and I feel quite sure you will see my point of view and understand. Do come and look us up sometime, its *years* since we saw you! Yours, Edwina.' As to Stafford Cripps, again, the two must have known each other, both members of the Labour Party, both involved, if at very different levels, in the movement for Indian independence. But why the mystery? And what was it that happened in Jermyn Street? Here, as on so many occasions before, my father remains, as I am sure he would have wished, the Invisible Man.

Acknowledgements

I would first and above all like to give wholehearted thanks to my sister, Caroline Shackleton: her recollections of my father and knowledge of our family history were invaluable to me, as was the substantial and generous assistance she unfailingly provided in my research. I would like to thank John Greenwald for the important help he gave me in tracking my father's career in California; and I am immensely grateful to Hugh and Heather Cameron, whose kindness and hospitality at the Yanko in New South Wales were crucial in helping me envisage my father's career as a jackeroo.

I would also like to put on record my gratitude to my late half-sister, Moorea, for her memories of her family and of her early years.

Documentary evidence of my father's life is regrettably sparse. He himself rarely wrote letters and when he did they were frustratingly uninformative. His most unguarded correspondence was undoubtedly with my mother, but those letters have never come to light; and he himself, after Maud Huntingdon's death, destroyed his own letters to his parents. To the Casati family papers, now the property of Silvio Berlusconi, it was not possible to have access, despite the kind interventions on my behalf of Avvocato Stefano Previti. Outside the family, one of the most important archives would have been that of Gavin Faringdon, a close friend of my father's and a man with a remarkable history of his own, but that, too, appears to have been destroyed.

For significant help with my research, I would like to give sincere thanks to the following:

Lucienne Allen, James Affleck, Michael Hardy and Kenneth Hillier at the Ashby-de-la-Zouch Museum, Prof. William Baker at Northern Illinois University, the Banco de México and the Diego Rivera Frida Kahlo Museums Trust, Thomasina Beck, the Benson Ford Research Center, Octavius Black, Fiona Cameron, Carol Cerf, Judith Curthoys at Christ Church College, Oxford, Maria Ketcham at the Detroit Institute of Art, Deborah Dewey, Dianna Dorman, Richard Dorment, David Freeman, Nicholas Glaser, John Gough, Sean Griffin, Jean Hannon Douglas, Pamela, Lady Harlech, Rosaleen Harrop, the Harry Ransom Center at the University of Texas at Austin, Penny Hatfield at Eton College Archives, Jane Holborow, Sean D. Noel at the Howard Gotlieb Archival Research Center in Boston, Christina Hughes-Onslow, Gayle M. Richardson at the Huntington Library in California, Tim Jeal, the Jerilderie Library in New South Wales, Laurie Henery at Jerilderie Shire Council, James Knox, Gillian Leeds, the London Library, Todd Longstaffe-Gowan, Jane Powell at the Marx Memorial Library, Jennifer McConnell, McMaster University in Hamilton, Ontario, Prince & Princess Massimo di Roccasecca, John McBratney, Samantha McEwen, Prof. William McGovern, Eunan McKinney, Karen Hendon and Helaine Glick at the Monterey Museum of Art, Caroline Moorehead, Countess Mountbatten of Burma, Constantia Nicolaides at the National Portrait Gallery, the Public Record Office of Northern Ireland, James Reeve, Rosaleen Remulji, Neil Robertson, Andrea de Robilant, Hermini Rohmursanto at the National Museum of Australia, Mark Rosenthal, the Countess of Rosse, William Laffan at Russborough House, Scot D. Ryersson, Barry Smith, René Solis, Peter Stansky, Kevin Leamon at the State Library of New South Wales, Syracuse University Special Collections Research Center, Hugo Vickers, Joel Villasenor, Alexander Waugh, Peter Waugh, Pericles Wyatt, Michael Yaccarino.

I owe a considerable debt to Alison McClean and to her informative thesis, *England's Rivera: the Lost Murals of Viscount John Hastings 1931–1938*, as well to her article, *Viscount Hastings: Radical Aristocrat* (*Praxis* no 156 Spring 2013).

I would also like to thank Rosa Rubner for allowing me to read her dissertation, "Art as a Weapon in the Political Struggle in 1930s Britain: Jack Hastings' Mural at the Marx Memorial Library."

As always, I am deeply indebted to my long-time friend and mentor, Julie Kavanagh, for her expert eye and critical perception; I have depended on her judgment for many years, and I only hope she will continue to be my first reader and most uncompromising critic. I am also immensely grateful to Prof. R. F. Foster and to Prof. T. F. Staley for their generosity in reading my text and making many valuable suggestions.

Finally I would like to thank, as always, my agent, Gill Coleridge, and also my publisher Robin Baird-Smith. It was he who encouraged me to take seriously the idea of writing this book and I owe a good deal to his patience and support.

Unless otherwise attributed, all photographs and all quoted material, including a number of untitled and undated press cuttings, are from the Hastings family collection.

About the Author

Selina Hastings is the author of four previous biographies, of Nancy Mitford, Evelyn Waugh, Rosamond Lehmann and Somerset Maugham.

She has been awarded the Marsh Biography Prize, the Spear's Award For Outstanding Achievement, and the Biographers' Club Award for Lifetime Services to Biography.

A Fellow of the Royal Society of Literature, she has been a judge of the Booker, Whitbread, British Academy, Ondaatje and Duff Cooper Prizes, and of the UK Biographers' Award.

Index

This index details the life of the 16th Earl of Huntingdon under the name Jack Hastings ('JH'), and elsewhere by events, names and places, and by his artwork.

Abbreviations

HGARC Howard Gotlieb Archival Research Center, Boston
       University
HRC   Harry Ransom Center, University of Texas at Austin
       Collection of Francis John Hastings, 16th Earl of
       Huntingdon
PRONI Public Record Office of Northern Ireland